LINCOLN CHRISTIAN COLLEGE AND SEMINARY

P9-DEO-003

PREACHING FROM CAMELOT TO COVENANT

ANNOUNCING GOD'S ACTION
IN THE WORLD

LINCOLN CHRISTIAN COLLEGE AND SEMINARY

PREACHING FROM CAMELOT TO COVENANT

ANNOUNCING GOD'S ACTION IN THE WORLD

William K. McElvaney

ABINGDON PRESS
Nashville

Preaching from Camelot to Covenant: Announcing God's Action in the World

Copyright © 1989 by Abingdon Press

All rights reserved.
No part of this work may be reproduced or transmitted in any form or by any means, electronic or mechanical, including photocopying and recording, or by any information storage or retrieval system, except as may be expressly permitted by the 1976 Copyright Act or in writing from the publisher. Requests for permission should be addressed in writing to Abingdon Press, 201 Eighth Avenue South, Nashville, TN 37202, U.S.A.

Library of Congress Cataloging-in-Publication Data

McELVANEY, WILLIAM K., 1928—
    Preaching from Camelot to covenant : announcing God's action in the world / William K. McElvaney.
        p.   cm.
    ISBN 0-687-33842-5 (alk. paper)
    1. Preaching.   I. Title.
BV4211.2.M34   1989
251—dc20   89-14948
                                                                            CIP

Scripture quotations unless otherwise noted are from the Revised Standard Version of the Bible, copyright 1946, 1952, 1971 by the Division of Christian Education of the National Council of the Churches of Christ in the U.S.A. Used by Permission.

Manufactured by the Parthenon Press at
Nashville, Tenessee, United States of America

To O. Eugene and Eva B. Slater
supportive friends, admired exemplars,
and trusted confidants for more than thirty-five years

6 40

13 March 1990

80536

Contents

Acknowledgments

The writing of a book commences long before the actual writing begins. Countless experiences, relationships, and reflections interact and eventually form the written page. From this complex web of influences come specific groups and persons to whom I am especially indebted.

The preaching of Marshall T. Steel confirmed the possibilities of the pulpit while I was in adolescent and young adult development, though in those years I never dreamed of personal pulpit occupance. The teaching of homiletics by the late Paul Scherer when I was a student at Union Theological Seminary during the year 1957–1958 made a lasting impression.

I owe more than I can say to the congregations of First United Methodist Church, Elma, Washington (Summer 1957); First United Methodist Church, Justin, Texas (1958); St. Stephen United Methodist Church, Mesquite, Texas (1959–1967); and Northaven United Methodist Church, Dallas (1967–1973). They have provided affirmation, encouragement, feedback, and patience beyond deserving for more than fifteen years of preaching. They have been my partners and faith colleagues in the "classroom" of the sanctuary.

Faculty colleagues of Saint Paul School of Theology and Perkins School of Theology have constituted the academic peer community in which my homiletical foundations and instincts have been further conceptualized, and I am grateful for them. I am particularly indebted to John Holbert, James Wharton, and Zan Holmes, Jr., for conversations and lectures which have shed light on a range of exegetical and homiletical issues. I am likewise appreciative of discussions through the years with Eugene Lowry and Laurence Wagley.

Kudos go to Perkins School of Theology students with whom I have shared homiletical wrestling, and especially to those in "the radical preaching groups" in which many of this book's issues have been addressed and demonstrated. I believe that they represent the brightest future for a profound and faithful pulpit. A hearty word of appreciation is due to three persons who as representatives of the laity have given time to classroom attendance in order to provide candid assessment of student sermons: Jerry Hobbs of St. Stephen United Methodist Church, and Anna Marie Harkey and Joanna Shields of Northaven United Methodist Church.

Fred Craddock was extremely gracious in providing insightful and penetrating reading of the manuscript. The final result is much the better for his gift of time and discernment, although of course the remaining shortcomings claim only the author as the rightful owner.

I am gladly forever indebted to Ann Ralston of the Perkins School of Theology staff who has compensated for my computer illiteracy by her unfailing graciousness, competence, and helpfulness in typing and processing several drafts of the manuscript. I also express deep appreciation to Ulrike Guthrie for her helpfulness in reading and processing the manuscript.

For the opportunity to test many of the concerns of the book in sermons, lectures, and workshops, I am especially grateful to the attendants of the Oklahoma Conference Ministers' Week (UMC) and of the Iliff School of Theology Graduate Lectures, to the participants of the Workshop on Preaching and Global Consciousness at Hendrix College, Conway, Arkansas, sponsored by the Steel Center for the Study of Religion and Philosophy and by the Episcopal and United Methodist bishops of Arkansas, as well as to the Arkansas Pastors' School (UMC) and the North Texas Conference (UMC).

Language is part of our formation as human beings and as Christians. Thus I seek to employ inclusive language throughout the text. Where using quotations, even if they are not as inclusive as I prefer, I have allowed the original language to remain.

William K. McElvaney
Perkins School of Theology
September 1988

Introduction

How can seminary students reflect the social conscience of the Bible for preaching in today's North American congregational life? How can pastors be faithful to the prophetic instinct in preaching and hope to remain in profound pastoral relationships with those whom we are called to serve? It is hardly news that our dominant cultural ethos does not encourage preaching that probes beyond apparent individual needs and hopes, or that the church itself does not necessarily reward even the faithful social conscience. In the pages that follow, I have called preaching that is only interested in these idealized personal concerns "Camelot" preaching. By contrast, "Covenant" preaching designates wider horizons, focusing on the social and global concerns of the Kingdom or Rule of God.

It is my privilege to provide leadership for a seminary preaching unit which I playfully call "How to Preach Prophetically and Keep your Appointment—Hopefully!" The contents of this book make up the kind of wrestling and discovery which have proven to be significant learning for both teacher and students. With all of the constant pressures to play it safe and to "speak to us smooth things" (Isa. 30), I am deeply concerned that our present and future pulpits throughout the land develop the conceptual and practical foundations for a hermeneutic and homiletic of sound community orientation. *To provide a stepping-stone for such a foundation is the purpose of this book.*

The concerns of *Preaching from Camelot to Covenant* are reflected in questions like these: How can we see inside our own biases and cultural osmosis which influence our biblical interpretation? What is our basic image or paradigm of preaching from where people are to where the gospel would lead us? What determines whether the preacher interprets the biblical text only for the personal lives of the congregation (Camelot) or for larger social and global issues as well (Covenant)? Could a preacher virtually never apply biblical texts beyond the perceived needs of the immediate congregation and still be regarded as a faithful biblical exegete by the generally accepted norms of exegesis? In our preaching, what does the Good News purport to save people *for*? What is the relationship between hermeneutics and the preacher's theology, imagination, and courage?

It is not my contention that these questions are absent in existing writings. Rather, my conviction is that they have not received adequate attention in the spate of literature frequently providing excellent resources in other dimensions of hermeneutical and homiletical disclosure. It is also my concern that literature about the social nature of preaching should meet the real world of weekly preaching in the parish as well as the conceptualization of the academy. My hope is that the present book is a contribution in that direction. Chapters 1 to 4 focus on the why, what, and how of preaching with a holistic social conscience. Chapters 5 and 6 provide an overview of the burdens and blessings of preaching per se.

No one claims that faithfulness to the whole gospel in preaching is easy or always comfortable. It never has been nor will it ever be. Preaching in North America during the last decade of the twentieth century and the opening years of the twenty-first century will certainly be no exception. Any perceptive analysis of the present preaching milieu in the North American church and society will acknowledge a widespread predisposition toward a defensive military mind-set, a self-protective view of economics regardless of consequences to others, and an overriding desire for a religion that guarantees individual success and status. We may have arrived at the time in U. S. history when the political party destined to be in office is the one—by whatever name—that successfully exploits the fears which are undergirding those issues. As preachers we would be naive not to discern the signs of current history.

At the same time God has given to the church a reservoir of human hopes and instincts in laity who yearn for the whole gospel. And most of all God has given to the church a story throbbing with life-giving images and symbols offering an alternative vision. The story gave life amid Pax Romana centuries ago. It will continue to call forth life in the most difficult circumstances of our time.

I believe there is ultimate joy and blessing in the unsurpassed privilege and responsibility of announcing the whole Word of God for the whole of life. The fact that such preaching is difficult and requires sensitivity to people, to text, and to self should beckon us to our best efforts and to ultimate dependence on amazing grace. The opportunity of a lifetime is before us. The time is at hand.

Part I

Preaching's Social Conscience

Chapter One

Preaching from Camelot to Covenant

In the den of our home is an artistic expression by Yaacov Agam, an Israeli artist. His work has been described as a modern day innovation of graphic art, a new visual orchestration unfolding in time, kinetic art which represents liberation from the fixed state of graphic art. He speaks of his art as motion and transformation, doing visually for the eye what music does for the ear.

Agam also describes his work as suggesting the ancient Hebrew concept of reality in which there is partial revelation, a coming into being rather than merely the perpetuation of the existing. The invisible endless reality behind things comes to mind in viewing Agam's work. His art, issuing forth in a fluidity of possible choices requiring reflection, calls for participation of the viewer as co-creator.

The particular work by Agam in our home is a lenticulated lithography called *Undersea Rainbow*. It consists of many circles and interacting shapes of varying color. The viewer does not look into a fixed, static scene, but rather participates in the art to become a part of the art. As the viewer moves, colors and forms change according to the viewer's shifting position and points of view. In other words what you see depends on where you stand.

Undersea Rainbow suggests something of the nature of biblical texts and our relationship as exegetes—richly layered material unfolding in time, requiring our participation, and a range of choices requiring reflection. The "viewer" does not simply act upon a static art (text) but must be drawn into it, viewing it from several points of view.

Undersea Rainbow has yet more to suggest. Even though it draws us into its rich movement and color on its own terms, the whole truth of the matter is that what we see depends on our point of viewing. Whether consciously or unconsciously, we bring to the viewing ourselves in relation to our culture, ourselves in relation to everything we have heard, seen, and experienced. Whether we like it or not and whether we acknowledge it or not, we inevitably bear hidden agendas, biases, and engage in selective filtering.

Biblical scholars have rightly made a great deal of the fact that preachers are interpreted and formed by the Word. Heaven help us—and those whom we are called to serve and represent—if that is not the case. However, it seems to me that not enough has been made of the fact that hermeneutics is always a two-way street in which the interplay of cultural osmosis and theological awareness constitutes the traffic. Indeed, the preaching process is a constant struggle between cultural osmosis and theological awareness. The preacher may observe the prescribed guidelines for exegetical work, yet fail to proclaim the gospel due to the presence of an unconscious a priori hermeneutic of persona and perspective. "Pre-existent" hermeneutic is the hidden joker in the deck of homiletical perspective.

As a seminary teacher I am always impressed with how much is already in place in the mind-sets of first-year students. The average age of entering students is just over thirty. So each student is a mixture of thirty years or so of cultural assumptions which impact theological, political, economic, and social positions. The seminary years usually result in many exciting and disturbing discoveries and the corresponding changes. Yet some of the old assumptions do not surrender quickly and easily, if at all. And once the academy with its "in" directions and pressures of grades for graduation gives way to the acculturated expectations of the provinces "out there," the former habits of experience frequently demand a new hearing and practice.

Cultural osmosis takes at least two forms. One is the faulty assumption that traditional biblical interpretations are *the* interpretations. To my knowledge, no one has underscored this more insightfully and forcefully than Justo Gonzalez and Catherine Gonzalez in their book *Liberation Preaching*.[1] As they insist, preachers need to develop a hermeneutical/exegetical suspicion in which the experience of "marginalized" people is taken into account. Traditional translations have reflected the perspective—and hidden agendas—of the translators. Lectionaries and commentaries are to be seen in a similar light.

Another form of cultural osmosis is our store of assumptions beyond those directly related to biblical study, which constantly influence the way we go about biblical hermeneutics. Unfortunately there is no assurance that our a priori hermeneutic, which inhabits all our presuppositions, will be reshaped and reformed in every respect by the gospel.

How else can we explain the need for the civil rights movement two decades ago, when large regions of the church, including seminary trained preachers, denied the clear claims of the gospel for an inclusive community? How else do we explain the advice of certain popular evangelists who counsel preachers to restrict God's Word from the pulpit to possibility thinking and personal issues and to avoid references to social justice? How else can we interpret "cheap grace"[2] sermons representing the equivalent of "quick fix" notions in society? Or moralizing homilies peddling "you get what you deserve" lessons warmed over from earning it the old-fashioned way?

A personal example of the "pre-existent" hermeneutic was the conversation between theology and politics in my own faith development. I came to seminary from a position with an oil company, a business degree from college, and a family professionally rooted in banking and finance.

Theological education was a major event in my life and in my faith journey. Even so, it took additional time for my theology to permeate my political viewpoint.

My political opinion was basically uninformed by any theological grounding. The assumptions were inherited from my family and tended to serve the interest of the privileged and the prosperous, or more literally, the security and advantage of me and "my kind." I "osmosed" it from the dominant values surrounding me. After I entered seminary I was confronted with a new hermeneutical base, an expanded view of history, and the challenges of liberation theology: different questions and different answers.

The old question, crudely but truthfully put, was "What's in it for me?" The new questions became, "How will it affect the poor and the marginal?" "What promotes cooperation and mature diplomacy?" These questions do not calcify into partisan politics. They bring biblically based theological questions to any and all political parties, platforms, and candidates. Sometimes the answers are difficult to discern and usually there are conflicting and competing values involved. That is the nature of politics. But at least the questions are motivated by, and rooted in, faith.

There is an assumption among some biblical scholars and those who write about preaching that knowledge of the Bible and of theological tradition assures that the gospel is understood and can be faithfully applied to human existence. For example: "The preacher who is rooted and grounded in *the* biblical [italics mine], theological tradition of the church—who has made that tradition part and parcel of his or her own being—is the preacher who understands the Gospel."[3]

The dilemma with this assumption is that there are *many* biblical and theological interpretations of tradition in conflict with each other, each claiming to be *the* tradition or at least the most correct one. We can say all we want about "letting the text speak for itself." But there is more to say. The voice of the text in its applicability for today inevitably depends on our theological presuppositions which in turn are influenced and in tension with cultural osmosis.

In the light of the struggle between cultural osmosis and biblical as well as theological awareness, the latter being themselves influenced by the former, what might our preaching look like today and in the immediate future? What might be some informing images and directions for preaching in our cultural setting?

Some Homiletical Clues and Contours: A Journey with Jacob

Ever since Alex Haley's *Roots*, people of every description have been scrambling to all kinds of genealogical resources. There are those sages who counsel us to leave well enough alone. No telling what you might turn up in the family genealogical closet. Undaunted I joined the search for the long lost ancestral tree.

Our name is Gaelic, part Scottish and part Irish. In reading the history of the Gaelic people my genes rose up and danced! After exhaustive research I traced my family roots all the way back to Jacob. Somehow I would not have connected McElvaney and Jacob, but that is the way it is. Who knows, maybe you are somehow in the same family tree. We shall see.

You remember Jacob, the quiet man, the apple of his mother's eye, dwelling in tents in contrast to brother Esau, the hairy hunter. Jacob, the smooth man—in more ways than one—the clever schemer with a penchant for mendacity, opportunistic with a crude mixture of motives . . . finessing the famished Esau for his birthright, and as though that were not enough, defrauding Esau and deceiving his aging father Isaac in order to secure the patriarchal blessing reserved for the first-born.

And you remember Jacob and the river Jabbok and the wrestling match that was to shape the rest of Jacob's life.[4] If you are a preacher, you have made a stab at this strange Genesis 32 text which Elie Wiesel compares with a mystical poem, mysterious from beginning to end, in which every question brings forth another.[5]

Consider the setting. Here is Jacob, alone yet not alone at night in the wilderness, running from Esau, yet destined to meet Esau on the morrow after all these years. Here is the post-Bethel Jacob, the aftermath of the long-ago rapture and rapport with God. If I were a filmmaker I would roll a flashback at this point, revealing the dream at Bethel representing the honeymoon of the Covenant with God. Jacob's ladder, we call it. We have climbed it in song countless times. Traffic between heaven and earth. Angels of God ascending and descending. Remember the mountain top inspiration, Jacob? Then you knew firsthand God's promise to uphold you through thick and thin in a Covenant relationship.

Now the inevitable ongoing journey. Memory of God's promise weakens with time. This is Jacob up against it, in flight from self and life. Esau is coming with four hundred men. Jacob hopes against hope that Esau's memory has grown dim. But just in case, Jacob's gift of appeasement has been sent. But will it be sufficient? Two hundred she-goats and twenty he-goats, two hundred ewes and twenty rams, thirty milch camels and their colts, forty cows and ten bulls, twenty she-asses and ten he-asses. Quite a tribute! This is, if you will, Jacob in an uncertain appointment, weary and out of schemes, going through the motions, for whom the rush of blood at ordination and first sermon has slowed to a trickle, to a tedium instead of a *Te Deum*.

The Wrestling God

We are told of a nocturnal wrestling match between Jacob and an inscrutable stranger. Von Rad says "the word 'man' [as used in the text] is open to all possible interpretations."[6] Brueggemann remarks that the text's "rich expository possibility is based in part on its lack of clarity!"[7] What are we to make of this struggle?

To begin with, the text seems to be saying in part that life does not come to us clearly marked or neatly labeled. It is not clear with whom or with what we are wrestling when momma dies, when Joe loses the only job he has ever had, when baby Joan is stillborn, when Wayne and Betty separate after twenty-seven years, or when carcinoma threatens to incarcerate life. Are we wrestling with God or devil, friend or foe, advocate or adversary?

Note that Jacob asks the name of his antagonist—or is it protagonist? In many ancient societies naming carried great power, including control over the identity of persons and gods. Jacob is answered by a question, "Why do you ask my name?" The identity of the unknown aggressor indeed seems to shift. The biblical text uses the word *ish*, man, also translated *someone* by some scholars. According to Wiesel, the Midrash and the commentators elevate the naming to the rank of angel.[8] And Jacob, who should know as well as anyone, continues the identity progressions: "I have seen God face to face, yet my life is preserved" (Gen. 32:10). Earlier in the text the wrestling partner confirms Jacob's appraisal by asserting, ". . . you have striven with God *and* with men, and have prevailed" (vs. 28).

It may be that there is at least a symbolic connection here with Jacob's exclamation upon encountering Esau at the rising of the sun (ch. 33). ". . . for truly to see your face is like seeing the face of God, with such favor you have received me" (vs. 10). Possibly this is the ingratiating element of Jacob's fear but it cannot help but suggest that to wrestle with human relationships is to wrestle with God and vice versa. Such a reading would certainly be true to the genius of Hebrew faith.

What else may be disclosed in the wrestling? Is there a gift of grace, that is, a saving reality, and if so, saving us for what? Sometimes the church seems to claim that the word of faith will remove trials and tribulations, that grace will protect you from failure and hardship, and that we were meant to be the "Society for the Promotion and Preservation of the Privileged and Prosperous, at Ease in Zion." God wants you to be successful, we hear. Before we become too smug in casting stones at television evangelists, we had better confess that the desire for such grace lurks in us all. I yearn for simple answers in preparing sermons, but there are none. If we live with impending sorrow or tragedy, do we not desire simplicity and swiftness of sure solution? If you wait for the doctor's report, do you not long for a clean and clear bill of health? Do we not yearn for a simple once-and-for-all solution to the Damocles Sword of nuclear threat, like magically turning into reality the bumper sticker that says—Nuclear Weapons: May you rust in peace!

We wrestle with life; life wrestles with us. We have a deep yearning for the grace of quick solutions, and when none comes, we are tempted to conclude—along with many in our society—that there is no grace, no God at all.

Except in moments of faith, do not we who define ourselves as church, *also* cry out with those who define themselves otherwise? God will provide the necessary grace, you say. Grace? Why, grace did not prevent the Holocaust nor other historical genocides. Grace does not protect countless women and children (and sometimes men) from being battered and abused. Grace does not intervene to prevent earthquakes and natural disasters that level whole populations. Powers and principalities that crush millions of people in poverty and hunger seemingly go unnoticed by the supposed dispenser of grace. The suffering of the innocent abounds unabated. Does grace abound also?

Another option offers itself to Jacob in this paradigm of life described as a wrestling match. As I see it, it is a live option for preaching. The author—shall we say evangelist?—tells a story and offers a choice. And the story is that grace is usually wrapped around a wrestling match with life, around ambiguity, complexity, and uncertain outcomes. The story is: there is an "Ultimate Reality"—the "Not-me, the Not-you, the Not-all-of-us-put-together"—who meets us in the wilderness, in our aloneness, at the river Jabbok as well as in Bethel, who wrestles with us to bring us to blessing, who will not let us alone, who loves us enough to wrestle with us, who encounters and engages us. This "Ultimate Reality" is not the god of the Deists, who creates and takes a cosmic walk, but the wrestling event-full God of Israel, the God of life and history. There is something of G. K. Chesterton's *God of Earth and Altar* here: smite us and save us all.[9] It is the Inevitable-Irrepressible One with whom we have to relate whether we like it or not. Do we sense a whiff of incarnation in the Wrestling One who engages us?

The Bible has an unsettling way of describing life without any cover, yet brimming with hope. It is not the task of preaching to provide a covering veneer that removes ambiguity and struggle in the name of a placebo god. Preaching that exempts grace and faith from the ambiguity and struggle of the wrestling match promises too much, even in the name of Jesus Christ. For even the incarnational disclosure of God's love in Jesus Christ, even this ultimate assurance and acceptance and empowerment does not preclude Christians from wrestling to receive this gift of all gifts in the vicissitudes of daily living and decision making. Preaching that does not tell the story of gift in encounter, of initiative from the "Not-me, the Not-you, the Not-all-of-us-put-together," is preaching that promises too little.

Preaching the wrestling God is preaching something like a pre-venient grace: a grace that follows us in our fleeing; not a con-venient grace, but a confronting grace with a haunting refrain—live, come out, live. When you are tempted to quit on life, to quit on yourself, to give up on friends, or to lie down and die, the Hebrew God says, "Come out, come forth, and wrestle with me that I might give you a new lease on life and give you a blessing, perhaps a blessing for which you were not looking—become, wrestle and live."

Preaching does not initiate the wrestling. That is already happening in the lives of the congregation. Preaching hopes to interpret the wrestling, to draw life from it, to point to a hidden transcendent yet incarnational depth of hope and courage in the encounter, to open our eyes and ears for what is given. A blessing! But what kind of blessing?

The Renaming God

Jacob refuses to disengage unless he is given a blessing. The RSV text says, "I will not let you go unless you bless me." Vintage Jacob: always on the "make" for a blessing. A finely honed instinct for leverage, an advantage when the bargaining gets sticky. "Give me a blessing, God. Make it right." Given that posture, not letting go was the biggest mistake Jacob ever made, the surprise of a lifetime. The Wrestling God turns out to be the Renaming God. Jacob, the Grasper, the Supplanter, becomes Israel, the one who will forever strive and wrestle with God. The meaning of the blessing and birthright is turned upside down. Jacob becomes the father of the twelve tribes of Israel and is signed up almost against his will for a larger story and journey by initiative from elsewhere. This is not what Jacob had in mind.

It is as though God said, "You want a blessing, do you? Well, it's yours! You will have the blessing, the birthright of my Covenant. You will have the promise of my faithfulness and affirmation—and you will have the confronting, demanding relationship of my claim and purpose that always attends the promise of the Covenant. This *is* the blessing!" Is this the mystery of what Christian theology has come to call a justifying and sanctifying grace, a grace for us, yet in us and through us? A grace that frees us for "somebody-ness" for others? A grace that renames us for a new destiny, that restores us as we are "restoried" in the larger vision and work of God?

While the renaming itself is isolated and evidently unknown in the following narratives in Genesis, it is enormously suggestive for faith and for preaching.

What happened to Jacob is fundamental to Christian preaching. For what God is doing—wrestling and renaming—is the Genesis and the Revelation of preaching. And what God is doing is wrestling us into a larger vision, an eternal story, an ultimate promise and claim. Every vita, every biography, every autobiography, from Genesis to Revelation, of those who came into faith, is the story of the initiative of God, restoring human beings for an alternative and altered script: Moses minding his own business and tending sheep; Jonah; the peasant woman Mary, and Joseph, her betrothed; Zacchaeus. The story is always different in particulars but the same in intent and telos. For in the wrestling and renaming, God is asking us, "Is life finally only our story, or is life a larger story of the broadest connections?"

Let me see if I can contour it this way. When we were children we naturally played games of make-believe. In make-believe—the power and freedom of imagination— you could become anyone, real or imaginary. Nowadays, it might be Superman, Wonderwoman, Luke Skywalker, Chris Evert Lloyd, Magic Johnson. In my childhood it was the likes of Tom Mix, Mandrake the Magician, Dick Tracy, or some characters of my own creation! Shades of Jonathan Livingston Seagull! You could break all of the barriers and limits of human finitude, even time and space. The sky was literally the limit.

When we become adults we continue to play a version of make-believe just because we are human beings. We think about what we want to be and to become in life. We become our own futurist, and we inevitably put together a kind of blueprint, both short-range and long-range, toward which we imagine our life will develop. What does your blueprint look like? I expect it includes someone to love and to be loved by, in marriage or in friendship or both. I suspect it includes some dimensions of recognition and achievement. Most of us like someone to say along the way, "Hey, you did a good job. That was needed and made a difference." We usually put good health in our blueprint. We think about a secure financial situation, even "megabucks." We think about travel. We imagine the good life and the fulfillment of a host of other hopes, dreams, and plans.

Our blueprints do not include the tragic dimension. And why should they? After all, who wants adversity and affliction? Who hopes for suffering or failure? And so we inevitably gather together in our minds, whether in discursive or narrative form, an idealized future of success and happiness and well-being. I call this idealized mental picture our *Camelot*.[10] It is our special world that we think about and concoct in our imagination.

Then along comes real life, not merely as we imagine it, but as we experience it. The real bumps up against the ideal. As we all learn, the *footprints* of life do not always

match the *blueprints* of our Camelot. Adjustments and al-
terations become necessary. The erosion and fading of Camelot is the formula for mid-life and other life-stage crises,
precipitating an anxious search for security and certainty
of approval and "somebody-ness." And whenever a society
experiences the disintegration of familiar moorings, the
shifting of the foundations, challenges to familiar forms of
authority—whether for better or worse—then the yearning
for unambiguous answers and authority figures, whether
in persons or in systems, becomes all the stronger.

A key issue for preaching today, with regard to content,
is whether we speak mainly Camelot language or a language beyond Camelot. To be sure, God is not disinterested
in our imagined personal Camelots. The biblical witness is
clear enough that God rejoices with those who rejoice—as
long as it is not rejoicing born of greed or insensitivity to
others—and weeps with those who weep. God cares for our
unselfish hopes and dreams and is our Emmanuel companion in times of joy and in moments of stress and sorrow.
God is at the wedding feast. God is by our side at the grave.
We are told that not a sparrow falls beyond divine encom-
passing.

It is not that our personal lives and our private dreams
are too insignificant for God's attention or care. We could
persuasively claim that the supreme worth of each and
every individual is the most remarkable feature of the New
Testament and of the ministry of Jesus Christ. No, it is not
that God has taken a walk from our personal blueprints. It
is that God has more in mind for us all than our privately
imagined Camelots, and that "more" is basic to Christian
preaching in whatever form it takes. Frequently God does
not save us, touch us, reach out to us, interact with us in
the ways we would have imagined, chosen, or preferred.
We have only to talk with Abraham and Sarah, Moses,
Jonah, Mary, Paul, or almost any other biblical figure from
Genesis to Revelation to be reminded that God has always
been full of surprises, some to our liking and some not, that
God has a broader and deeper story in mind than our
private Camelots.

In short, God seeks to save us to become our deepest and truest selves for God and for others, to restore us to our intended purpose in community. This greater reality is known as *Covenant*, more life-giving and more freeing than even the best of our imagined blueprints.

The *question* today for the church—and thus for all of us who are called to be preachers—is whether we will major in Camelot language or whether we will draw deeply from Covenant language. An ancient epigram from an author to his translator said: "The work you recite is mine, O translator/But when you recite it badly, it begins to be yours."[11]

When we traffic mainly in Camelot language, in the consumer interest of the individual, does not preaching begin to be our word rather than the wrestling, renaming Word of God?

Covenant preaching is all the more essential today due to the particular version of Camelot theology preached by the "electronic church." Its influence is enormous, and it is possibly a judgment on the rest of the church in somehow failing to reach lonely and frightened people. Electronic Camelots tend to prey (p-r-e-y) on crass images of prosperity and success, even suggesting that this is what God is about in calling us to faith. There are some in the church who would say, "God is the guarantor of your personal Camelot. Have faith and everything will come out the way you want it." Success guaranteed. You can hear it in some churches around town.

In *Letters and Papers from Prison*, Dietrich Bonhoeffer gave the most profound description of a Christian I have ever heard. A Christian, Bonhoeffer claims, is one who deliberately seeks to identify with the suffering of Christ and human beings in the world.[12] This is not Camelot talk, at least not of the usual variety. This is Covenant talk. Camelot is rooted in the habits of individualism. Covenant is connected with a long line of risk takers who could not define themselves apart from sinners, sufferers, and Samaritans. Covenant is the language of gift; Camelot is the language of possession. Covenant talk is people talk, community talk, in which justice, peace, and shalom are the pearls of great price. The Covenant blueprint is flexible and fluid, yet anchored in special responsibility rather than special privilege, a vision of global well-being and neighbor-oriented purpose; namely, to alleviate human suffering and to elevate human suffrage.

The wrestling and renaming of Jacob seems to suggest that he must wrestle with God on the way to meet his estranged brother. Covenant theology is wrapped around the fundamental discrepancies and contradictions of the human situation. Yet Covenant theology is always a "therefore" theology, moving from God's grace to the inseparable claim on our lives by which we are motivated to become servants of justice, liberation, and reconciliation. By preaching from a Covenant hermeneutic I do not mean to suggest a generalized thematic approach negligent of the particularities of various biblical texts. I mean rather to suggest that within the Christian community we need to be ever conscious of the temptation to remake the gospel in our own image. The Scripture itself is of course the source of a so-called Covenant hermeneutic if we only let it speak to us in ways that overcome our cultural osmosis, our conceptual traps, as Elizabeth Dodson Gray[13] puts it.

An informing image of preaching content today is that of a representative people called to be a sign of God's love and justice. *Covenant talk seeks neither to neglect nor to destroy the Camelot of individual longing but to redefine Camelot.* Covenant grace transforms Camelot into a broader perspective, from me and mine to a new ambition of compassion and concern for the forgotten. Through the Covenant of unconditional love we are freed for others and the new Camelot begins to coincide with the Kingdom or Rule of God. Covenant is God's subversive solidarity with hurting, oppressed people, a summons, as Dorothee Sölle suggests, to take up our cross by breaking neutrality and becoming proactive with God on behalf of oppressed peoples.[14] In traditional Christian terminology we know this as conversion. And when preaching is an agent for that transformation, we call it truly reformed, truly evangelical, and truly catholic.

Let it be noted that the Good News of Covenant preaching is not suited to a badgering, authoritarian style, nor to the spirit of pusillanimity. We extend bold invitations to taste and to savor, to enjoy, to wonder, to connect, to doxologize the One who is the Giver and Receiver of all life.

Today there is no task for preaching more compelling and more challenging than making the distinction between cheap grace and costly free grace. Is there room in Camelot for the God who embraces pain? For a gospel of the everywhere Exodus-Easter God whose Covenant has to do with causes as well as effects, with power and politics and principalities as well as prayer and personal piety? For loving one's enemies? Is there room in Camelot for a God who loves us enough to disturb us, and whose blessed disturbance is our unrecognized profoundest hope?[15] Does Camelot Inn have a room for the grace and truth of the Covenant God in which the assurance of victory is the victory of living for that truth?

Regardless of sermonic form, whether propositional or narrative, if we do not exegete both text and the congregational and cultural context from a Covenant hermeneutic rather than a Camelot hermeneutic, our preaching may be popular and may result in numerical church growth, but it will not conform the church to the image of the Vulnerable-Victorious One in whose name we preach. Only if the informing image of preaching, as well as other dimensions of the church's being, is the image of the Crucified-Risen Lord (which I take it is what we mean when we say, "Preach Christ") will there be joy in heaven and a faithful church on earth.

The Wounding God

There is one more piece to this jumbled-up puzzle of a text in Genesis 32 as far as preaching is concerned. We are told that Jacob's thigh was put out of joint and that he limped away from the wrestling encounter.

What do we make of this wound? It certainly does not fit our image of God as comforter, of a balm in Gilead, of Jesus the Great Physician who heals. Some would think this text is too primitive to be accorded a place in enlightened

Christian interpretation, that it ought to tuck its tail between its hind legs and slink off to the junkyard of Old
Testament texts that do not quite make it with our sophis-
ticated culture. I am going to suggest that the wounding
cannot be separated from the wrestling and the renaming,
either in life or in preaching. In fact, the Wrestling God,
the Renaming God, is also the Wounding God.

*Could Jacob's wound be the wound which offers wholeness to
us all?* Not a wound that automatically makes us whole, but
which offers us wholeness in the security of God's purpose?
There is given to us—or should I say inflicted upon us—a
heightened awareness calling us to lean into the world's
pain. Does the gospel wound us and yet heal us through
the vulnerability of self-giving love?

This vulnerability is not to be interpreted as an en-
forced relationship which characterizes oppressor-op-
pressed relationships. This language and the images of
sacrificial love and vulnerability have too often been used
to justify abuse and unjust power relations. Rather, the
vulnerability lifted up here is the gift of God to be freely
and intentionally chosen on behalf of others.

Could creative dislocation be the movement of grace?[16] God's
movement dislocates our self-serving assumptions, puts out
of joint our professional pride and our neglect of others,
and puts question marks around our self-contrived securi-
ties, offering freedom in the mind and the way of the Christ.

*Could Jacob's wound be the wound through which pours the
life of God?* Not just any God, but the God concealed and
yet revealed in strange and lonely places, like Bethel and
the Jabbok, making nowhere somewhere and nobody some-
body; like "East of Eden" and the westside of the wilderness;
like the color purple and the polychromatic parade of red
and yellow and black and brown and white; the God who
is identified with a wash basin and towel, in bread broken
and blood poured out; who comes off crosses and out of
tombs; whose being, whose coming and going and always
coming again as the Vulnerable-Victorious One, the Suffer-
ing-Sovereign One is the great mystery of existence—
whose life pours through Jacob's wound. Are there intima-
tions of the cross with its strength and weakness in this

supposedly primitive Hebrew text? Of *The Magnificent Defeat*, as Buechner put it?[17]

Could Jacob's wound be our Achilles heel in reverse? Vulnerability on the unprotected heel of Achilles, the great Greek warrior in the Trojan War, was the occasion of his death. By contrast, our wound of vulnerability is the occasion of life and deepest joy, our passport into the realm of the resurrection. It is the indelible *mark* of all those who have been wrestled and renamed and reclaimed, the signature of a perfecting grace. And it is the indelible *Word* that we are called to preach in the name of God.

Camelot, Covenant, and Kingdom

As I have described Camelot, our blueprint for life, it will be obvious that it is made up of many dreams and hopes. Some are relational, others are materially oriented and yet others are deeply personal. Some are virtually universal, such as being loved, loving someone else, and good health. Others are perhaps peculiar or unique to the one holding the blueprint. I can imagine Camelots that are not intentionally selfish though quite limited and unaware of inherent advantages and disadvantages hidden within systems. Others are covertly self-serving and opportunistic to the detriment of others. For most of us, our Camelots are probably a mixture of decency and less admirable qualities, especially when considered on a global basis.

The "Wesleyan Watch Night Service" in one of its present forms articulates the ambiguity of our Camelot-Covenant connection: "Christ has many services to be done; some are easy, others are difficult; some bring honor, others bring reproach; some are suitable to our natural inclinations, and temporal interests; others are contrary to both. In some we may please Christ and please ourselves; in others we cannot please Christ except by denying ourselves."[18]

So it is with our Camelots. In the gospel our Camelots are both yes and no. But the Watchnight Covenant continues, "Yet the power to do all these things is assuredly given us in Christ, who strengthens us."[19] Thus there is hope in the journey from Camelot to Covenant. The difficult challenge of preaching is to serve as a midwife for the journey.

One more assertion about Camelot cries out for attention. What many of us take for granted materially as a kind of minimum for an expanding Camelot constitutes an unfulfilled aspiration in the Camelot hopes for the majority of the world's people. This is by way of saying that the essentials of Camelot for a decent life free from hunger and disease and poverty cannot be separated from Covenant values and the Kingdom or Rule of God.

Without intending to provide a detailed biblical treatise on the term covenant, it is nevertheless desirable to indicate with more precision the use of the term herein. In the New Testament there are thirty-three instances of the term *diatheke*, translated as covenant. Of the thirty-three occasions nine are in Pauline literature, seventeen in Hebrews, four in the Synoptics, two in Acts, and one in Revelation.[20] Since Christians today, whether clerical or lay, are most familiar with the eucharistic language of covenant in the New Testament, I will focus our attention there.

The *Interpreter's Dictionary of the Bible* suggests that the narratives of the Last Supper (Matt. 26:28; Mark 14:24, Luke 22:20; 1 Cor. 11:25) provide evidence that for a time at least the early Christians regarded themselves as a covenant community bound together in Christ, and that "this covenant is a most free, creative reinterpretation of the older traditions."[21] "The point is that the blood, or death, of Jesus establishes the new *diatheke* (covenant) and the wine represents it."[22]

The relationship to Christ is both the content and the obligation of the New Covenant, so that the decalogue is summed up in the love command of Jesus and yet constitutes a gift from God.

The concept of preaching from Camelot to Covenant could also be translated from Camelot to Kingdom or Rule of God.

> The new covenant is correlative to the kingdom. As the kingdom expresses God's lordship, the covenant expres-

ses the saving will of God that constitutes its goal and
insures its validity.

. . . The *diatheke* is God's disposing, the mighty declara-
tion of his will in history, by which he orders the relation
between himself and us according to his saving purpose,
and which carries with it the authority of the divine
ordering."[23]

From Camelot to Covenant and Kingdom is the push
and pull of preaching. It will save us *from* stagnation and
decay of the soul and *for* our intended participation in the
life of God and thus for God's work in the world.

Chapter Two

Theology and Experience for Covenant Preaching

"Are you free to preach the gospel?" This was the question addressed to Nico Smith by Karl Barth during Smith's visit to Basel in 1963. The question never left Nico Smith, haunting him for years.

After several years, a crisis of conscience led the Afrikaner Smith to resign as a minister of the Dutch Reformed Church of South Africa as well as from his professorship of missiology at the Afrikaner University of Stellenbosch. Accepting a call from the black Dutch Reformed Church in Mamelodi, Nico Smith now lives in the black township where he and his wife have become a sign of reconciliation, preaching and living a message of hope. In spite of ostracism from former white friends in South Africa, the Smiths bring whites and blacks together in Koinonia groups amid the apartheid society. He speaks of "a deep peace of heart!"

Karl Barth's question to Nico Smith is applicable to all of us who represent the preaching ministry. "Are you free to preach the gospel?" Nico Smith thought so at the time. Later he became convinced that he was not free to preach the gospel, that he was blindly bound to the presuppositions of his society and to his own vested interest. As his reflections on the gospel deepened, he slowly began to challenge his social conditioning, his "cultural osmosis" as I have been calling it.

Since in the United States we live and preach in a "free" society it could be tempting to assume that we are indeed free to preach the gospel. In the sense that we enjoy freedom of speech and freedom to exercise the right of social criticism, we are free to preach the gospel. Yet our preaching is constantly conditioned by the fact that we are social beings, influenced by the impact of society on us and thus on our theological presuppositions which undergird our preaching. Barth's question is not only about the freedom of speech in a repressive society but also about the freedom of the preacher in relation to the gospel in any society.

What are some of the factors, both theological and experiential, which free us to preach from Camelot to Covenant, to become more aware of our hermeneutical presuppositions, to relate our preaching to the vital issues of our day in ways faithful to the gospel?

Theology for Covenant Preaching

Like most seminary graduates I was not sure what I was doing, at least in a deeply reflective sense, during the initial year or so of preaching in the early 1960s. This is more clear to me now than it was then, yet hindsight convinces me that I had by and large the right instincts and priorities for preaching content. Two comments from parishioners would be somewhat representative of the time from the 1960s to the early 1970s in relation to my preaching. One was, "Your preaching proclaimed God's grace in both the yes and the no of life, so that we could hope to find a yes in the noes."

This word of assurance is what Brueggemann has called a stabilizing interpretation which provides equilibrium.[1] In the vernacular of homiletics it offers comfort to the afflicted, the possibility of new beginnings in old endings. The Good News that we can live again in spite of all the in-spite-ofs is rooted and grounded not in pollyanna human optimism but in God's unconditional love and empowering grace. The God of Jesus Christ is a God of comfort and companionship in the noes of life.

The other comment was this: "Your preaching is sometimes hard to swallow, but always nutritious." (Lest this

appear to be self-serving, I hasten to add that not everyone
agreed with the second half of the statement!) Even though
my formal theological education in the 1950s was centered
in white male North American and European theologians
(Barth, Brunner, Bultmann, Bonhoeffer, Tillich, the Nie-
buhrs, Daniel Day Williams, with "exceptions" like D. T.
Niles and Georgia Harkness), the experience was not without powerful testimony and rootage in themes of justice,
human dignity, and a gospel concerned for the transformation of both souls and systems. This dimension of my
preaching was the element of discontinuity with prevailing
cultural values, touching on issues of racial discrimination,
peace with justice, and public concern for the downtrodden.
Brueggemann calls this a genre of preaching that presents
"a world of transformation,"[2] or in pulpit parlance, afflict-
ing the comfortable. Through the years, I have believed
that moving from Camelot to Covenant in the pulpit is
sustained by a theology of both comfort and challenge.

The Foolishness of God

For better or worse most preachers have a gospel within
the gospel that serves both as a beacon light and a lens or
filter through which the metabolism of biblical faith is perceived. For me, a basic image in preaching has been the
"foolishness of God" by which conventional wisdom is reversed (1 Cor. 1:18–31). This "underdog" theology is typical
of the movement of God in history and has informed my
hermeneutic throughout most of my preaching efforts.[3]

The reversal of societal norms by the "foolishness of
God" resymbolizes our life vision, exploding our common
assumptions and offering an alternative world view. I believe it is this redemptive absurdity which subverts the
cultural myth-story of inevitable throw-away relationships,
technological waste, chemical and electronic drugs, ration-
alism without moral integrity or compassionate warmth.
The Crucified-Risen One is at odds with instant gratification, unlimited material acquisition, and the necessity of
promoting international enmity in order to insure a huge

military system while our cities decay, people hurt for health care, and the plight of the poor worsens.

If the gospel does not call forth a story radically different from the world around us, why preach? When the church loses the sense of the gospel's absurdity in relation to the way things are, we become acculturated to a domesticated religion of benign spirituality. We become accommodated with little reservation to the values of our economic class, our political party, our social club, our national ethos; in other words, well-adjusted to a Camelot of our own devising. We lose the wonder, the challenge, the risk, and yes, even the comfort offered by the larger story called Covenant. For me it has been the disparity between the gospel and reality that has fueled much of my preaching.

The Reign of God: The Reversal of Human Wisdom

The Reign of God is a dominant guide, an all-encompassing image which can unite our total ministry in a profound biblical framework. It continues the central message of Jesus as our theological motif for preaching. In *Announcing the Reign of God* Mortimer Arias has provided an especially helpful study of the gift, hope, and challenge of the Kingdom or Reign of God.

> . . . The kingdom of God, announced by Jesus, is multi-dimensional and all-encompassing. It is both a present and a future reality. It has to do with each individual creature and with the whole of society. It was addressed initially to "the lost sheep of the house of Israel," but was destined for "the whole world" and to "the end of the earth." It embraces all dimensions of human life: physical, spiritual, personal and interpersonal, communal and societal, historical and eternal. And it encompasses all human relationships—with the neighbor, with nature, and with God. It implies a total offer and a total demand. Everything and everybody has to be in line with it: "Turn away from your sins and believe the Good News" (Mark 1:15, TEV) of the kingdom of God.[4]

At the same time Arias reminds us that we have reduced and distorted the Reign of God to suit our own interests. Our own renderings of the Kingdom turn out to be whittled-down versions.

> Sometimes, like some church fathers in the Middle Ages, we have reduced the kingdom to a transcendent sphere outside the realities of this world and the struggles of history. At other times we have reduced the kingdom to the institutional and visible kingdom of the church. At still other times we have recovered the apocalyptic facet of the kingdom and preached a catastrophic end of this world with an imminent second coming. Or we have taken refuge in a reduced kingdom of our inner experience of salvation or the baptism of the Holy Spirit without any reference to Christ's lordship over the totality of life or to the social and cosmic dimensions of the kingdom of God. Or we have reduced the eschatological kingdom announced by Jesus Christ to a historical kingdom identified with a particular scheme of revolution and social order. And all the time we have identified our reduction of the kingdom with the whole, at the cost of the other dimensions.[5]

> . . . That time has come: the Scripture with the "subversive memory of Jesus," and the Holy Spirit with its antiamnesiac ministry—the two great subverters of history and the church—are calling us to recover the fullness of the biblical gospel of the kingdom to be announced to our generation.[6]

We easily forget that every time we pray the Lord's prayer we pray for the will ("kingdom") of God to be done *on earth* as in heaven. Thus we pray for God's initiative to bring a redeemed society, a world order of well-being and wholeness (shalom), of peace with justice. We symbolically act out the coming-of-the-Kingdom vision in the eucharistic meal where all are of sacred and equal value and where there is adequate food for all. In baptism we proclaim inclusion in the faith community whereby our final allegiance is to Jesus Christ and thus to Kingdom discipleship. A Philippine student in my preaching class told of a baptism in his country in which the pastor said, "You are baptized into the life, death, and resurrection of Jesus Christ. You are also baptized into the struggle for liberation and justice for your brothers and sisters."

Preaching that centers in the Reign of God will have a strong indicative of God's all-encompassing grace. The Reign of God is an image of transcendence becoming both immanent and imminent. It points to who God is and what God is doing. In Jesus Christ we see the activity of God disturbing, healing, reconciling, and liberating. At the same time the Reign of God is announced, we are called to become participants in the already present and yet coming Reign of God. There is an imperative to watch, to wait, and to order our lives accordingly. God's coming Reign over-throws all other allegiances in the ultimate sense. It is both gift and demand, promise and claim. What better frame-work for preaching?

The Reign of God reverses human wisdom with an assortment of images calling for an entirely new perspec-tive. These images bear the appearance of foolishness, weakness, and surprise. "Every valley will be lifted up, and every mountain and hill be made low" (Isa. 40:4). ". . . many that are first will be last, and the last first" (Mark 10:31). "He who finds his life will lose it, and he who loses his life for my sake will find it" (Matt. 10:39). "For everyone who exalts himself will be humbled, and he who humbles himself will be exalted" (Luke 14:11). Each passage deserves study in its particular context in order to arrive at its meaning, yet all indicate that the wisdom of the world is reversed and turned upside down.

Symbols of the Reign of God

The symbols of the Reign of God are similarly beyond human comprehension. Crib, crown of thorns, cross, empty tomb, bread, chalice and wine, towel, water—from begin-ning to unending the covenant story threatens the subver-sion of our culture story which is constantly forming and shaping our Camelots.

Would our consumer-oriented, acquisitive society make sense out of "the uncontrollable mystery on the bestial floor?"[7] It is difficult for our class-, race-, and status-conscious populace to warm to the idea of God indwelling a Jewish carpenter. It is difficult for our pleasure-seeking society to move toward a crucified leader, to believe that there is a higher and stronger power than Caesar, Pilate, Caiaphas, and all of us put together, a power stronger than death itself. Can we as preachers abide this mystery? It boggles the imagination. It is the "right stuff" of preaching.

For basic change to take place, either personal or societal, preaching needs to challenge the primary cultural symbols. I like to ask seminary students in preaching class to draw their perception of our culture's signs and symbols. They come up with dollar signs; number ones; people represented by stick figures climbing ladders or standing on other people or perhaps back to back facing in opposite directions; persons on escalators (going up, naturally); human figures gorging themselves with food and surrounded by a mass of goods; television sets bearing the culture's myth of success, power, and progress. Then we explore the symbols and images of the preaching story in contrast and go from there.

I am appreciative of the clear articulation by Thomas H. Troeger regarding the social power of story-myth and the need to revitalize religious imagination:

> Anyone, then, who is going to preach on social issues needs to understand the power of myth and its poetic language of image and symbols, their grip upon the landscape of the heart, and the enormous energies that they may release for good or evil.[8]

The Reign of God as a biblical, theological parameter for our preaching inevitably moves us from a basically individualistic perspective to a community orientation. Bluntly put, how can we claim to be saved as long as there are millions who suffer starvation, oppression, and subhuman lives? Reflecting on a world in which there is widespread child malnutrition, torture, violation of human rights, crime, drug addiction, consumerism and ecological neglect, Mortimer Arias exclaims, "It will not be enough to go around the world 'saving souls' with a census chart to get individuals to make 'instant decisions' for Christ."[9] And

who can forget Martin Luther King's testimony to the
interdependence of all life: "All (men) are caught in an
inescapable network of mutuality, tied in a single garment
of destiny."[10]

Saved to Participate

The late Rabbi Abraham Heschel, one of my favorite
authors, suggested that too many Christians are interested
in their own personal salvation rather than joining God in
the work of God in the world. What are we saved *for*? Have
not too many Christians either turned the gospel into a
cheap grace unrelated to Kingdom discipleship, as Arias
calls it, or else opted for some form of works righteousness?
I suspect that many of us have fallen into the trap of a
mercantile consumer religion suited to our own purposes
of security and self-protection.

> In going ahead with the Jesus Prayer . . . aren't you trying
> to lay up some kind of treasure? Something that's every
> . . . bit as negotiable as all those other more material
> things? Or does the fact that it's a prayer make all the
> difference? As a matter of simple logic, there's no dif-
> ference at all, that I can see, between the man who is
> greedy for material treasure . . . and the man who's
> greedy for spiritual treasure.[11]

Preaching needs to recover the balance in Paul between
both sides of the "therefore" that characterizes Paul's writing. John Wesley would call it justification and sanctification, the action of God both for us and in us. While we were
yet sinners Christ died for the ungodly. Therefore you are
free to affirm others and to work for their well-being. While
we were yet sinners, God's unmerited love was freely given.
Therefore you are called to be servants of peace and justice
in the name of Jesus Christ, the Prince of Peace and the
Champion of the World's Untouchables. Unfortunately one
side of the therefore has often been emphasized to the
detriment of the other side.

To be saved in the Covenant or the Kingdom of God is
to respond in faith to the gift of God's reign, to participate

in the work of God in the world, to find ultimate joy and meaning in being part of God's self-giving in the time of history we are given to live. And to say with Paul, "If we live, we live to the Lord, and if we die, we die to the Lord; so then, whether we live or whether we die, we are the Lord's. For to this end Christ died and lived again, that he might be Lord both of the dead and of the living" (Rom. 14:8–9).

Expanding the Horizons of Our Textual Interpretation

In this chapter we have considered two closely related theological frameworks which can inform our preaching: the "foolishness of God" and the Reign of God. Many other points of reference could and would be named by any group of preachers. For example, a theology of the Incarnation, the Word become flesh calling all of life under God's domain and influence, could inform our preaching gestalt. Others might focus on Easter as the central preaching paradigm from which all else derives. God is loose in the world and goes before us into every realm and sphere of creation: on the road, in the breaking of bread, in daily toil, in the paschal mystery of the Vulnerable-Victorious One as the backdrop of all our preaching.

My intention in calling for theological awareness is not to superimpose a general theme on the integrity of individual texts, even a good theme! Universal, abstract lessons or statements will not substitute well for the specific message of a text. But we do need to recognize that we *always* come to a text, or for that matter a topic, with existing presuppositions. With these filters and lenses we exegete the text, the congregation, and the world.

In the final analysis, what determines whether we interpret the text as applicable to individuals or as applicable to social issues and problems in present-day society, or to both? Granted that individuals and society are always in relationship so that neither can be adequately understood apart from the other, there are still choices to be made by the preacher's creative imagination.

"With a clear exegetical and theological understanding of the text and a clear identification of the situation of the congregation, the preacher makes the critical correlation of the text and the congregation."[12] Ronald J. Allen goes on to speak of the text as the decisive factor in prompting the preacher to determine the appropriate strategy for the sermon.

My concern, however, is *what determines* the possible connection of the text *beyond* the congregation to wider community and global issues. Could a preacher virtually never apply the text beyond the immediate congregation and still be regarded as a faithful interpreter according to normative notions of biblical exegesis? Due to poverty of imagination, benign neglect, pusillanimity of spirit, or a narrow theology of preaching, could a preacher simply apply texts to either individuals or to no wider context than the immediate local congregation and nonetheless be considered a true biblical exegete?

Let us take a couple of examples. One of my favorite passages through the years is Mark's version of the Gerasene demoniac (Mark 5:1–20). We have a dramatic narrative of Jesus' encounter with a man who has an unclean spirit and who lives among the tombs. Midway through the story, after the demoniac had been restored to his right mind, the neighborhood begins to beg Jesus to depart. The healed man begs to go with Jesus, but Jesus refuses him. High drama!

I doubt if there is anything inherent in the text itself which begs for a global interpretation. Would we not be acceptable exegetes simply to indicate the threat that a person in his or her right mind, that is, the mind of Christ, poses to our immediate neighborhood and let it go at that?

But suppose we decided to show instead the relevance of this part of the text to current world history. To show how this is not simply ancient history but to interpret how it relates locally *and* in Central America, in South Africa, in Northern Ireland. To show the global movement of the Holy Spirit in the lives of courageous persons who speak out amid repression, and how those in their "right minds" who speak out for reconciliation and justice and human decency are incarcerated, "kneecapped," or disappeared (in Central America *disappear* has become a passive verb).

By what criterion do we expand the horizons of interpretation? Perhaps some biblical scholar can point to inherent features in the text itself which escape my eye and ear. If so, attention needs to be paid. I suspect, however, that the criterion is usually the imagination of the preacher informed by a priori theological presuppositions; namely, that God is a global God of justice, calling the church and humanity at large to be participating agents in the foolishness or Reign of God; namely, that this passage is being recycled across the globe today and that our already present theology and ecclesiology calls for connecting the text to these global concerns.

Let us look at one other example. Turn to Matt. 9:18–34. Here we have a string of four healing stories: the ruler's daughter, the woman with a twelve-year hemorrhage, two blind men, and a dumb demoniac. Suppose we consider the final pericope in which the man without voice spoke as a result of the demon being cast out by Jesus. The Pharisees respond, "He casts out demons by the prince of demons" (vs. 34).

What shall we make of this? One option is to apply the healing to individuals in the congregation. The restoration of voice could be interpreted literally or in the sense of "somebodyness" and visibility reclaimed. We could point to a person restored to community. There is freedom from the past and for the future and getting on with one's life. Identity is not defined by "condition" but by relationship to God and the freedom thus represented.

Another option is to also relate this healing to what God is doing throughout the world. Jesus gives voice to the invisible ones, the silent ones. The response of the Pharisees is echoed in Latin America today and in other locations where people seek to be heard for the first time. The base ecclesial communities who organize for Bible study and interpretation relevant to the people's daily reality are labeled "Communist." According to military controlled governments and the branches of the church who support the status quo, they are in league with Marxist revolutionaries and have become ideological instead of theological communities. Silence the hope.

Again, by what measurement or canon of judgment do we decide to relate the text to situations beyond our own congregation and nation as well as to a local context? Is it not that it seems *natural* to the text and that we "see" this text in a larger perspective of texts pointing to a universal God, a global church, and a worldwide mission? The broader field of biblical texts has shaped a theological vision which is not licensed to force itself on the text but which is alert and sensitive to the relation between the text and the condition of the voiceless throughout the world. Covenant preaching expands and connects Camelot with the far reaches of the human condition and the divine response.

What I am saying is that our beliefs as to who God is, what God is about, and what the mission of the church is all about will inevitably influence the latitude and longitude of our textual exegesis. This is to affirm that biblical interpretation is first, last, and always a theological task.

Experience for Covenant Preaching

How can we as preachers move toward critical analysis and insight from our hidden agendas and interpretive biases? What are the counter moves to cultural osmosis which lead us from Camelot to Covenant preaching?

For me it has amounted in part to exposing present assumptions and positions to challenge and critique. Sometimes challenge and critique have come without my seeking it and at other times by my own volition. In the 1960s the civil rights movement brought to the surface our national disease of racism. In the 1970s the feminist movement exposed the two-way bondage of patriarchal systems and values. At about the same time Third World liberation theologies began to be published. All of these have sought to redefine Camelot into a transformed definition of "the good life."

Concerned more with the *systemic* than the *systematic*, and indebted to social sciences more than philosophies, the theologies of liberation represent voices of hope from the poor, the powerless, the marginal, the invisible segments of humankind. Orthopraxis—right action—becomes the litmus test rather than orthodoxy, transformation of the world becomes the verifiable measure of a faithful theology. Persons representing groups previously unheard are reading Scripture and analyzing societal conditions from the point of reference of the poor, the disadvantaged, the oppressed people of the world. Connections are being made between the conditions in which people live, the reasons for these conditions, and the liberating aim and action of God in history.

My Own Journey:
Liberation Theologies as a Faith Issue

In my own faith journey I have become greatly indebted to ethnic, feminist, and Third World theologians. I am convinced that one of the essential tasks of pastors and church leaders today is to listen to liberation theologians. Let me suggest why. I urge you, at least initially, not to think of liberation theologies as presenting a problem to be solved, nor a program or a project, but rather a pilgrimage, a passage into a deepening relationship with Jesus Christ, a spiritual journey into the paschal mystery of the Suffering One who is also the Sovereign One, the Vulnerable One who is also the Victorious One. If we approach liberation theologies initially as an imperative, we will quickly tire of the magnitude of the demand, and we will soon be looking for more comfortable and manageable projects.

However, if we become convinced that our relationship to Jesus Christ is closely connected with the outcast, the poor, the downtrodden, the invisible, then we are involved in a profound and abiding *faith* issue which can gift us, and to be sure, challenge us all our days. In the final analysis I

am convinced that liberation theologies offer all of us, as
the old spiritual puts it, "a closer walk with Thee." After
all, the themes of liberation theologies are basically inherited from the Hebrew prophets, the Gospels, and the
early church. How could it not inform our preaching?

In 1975 Robert McAfee Brown gave a keynote address
at the World Council of Churches in Nairobi, Kenya. I recall
reading his basic message in the church press, namely, that
Jesus' message of good news to the poor constitutes bad
news for the affluent, and I remember thinking that this
was and is true without any question.[13] But as I continued
to reflect on this truth, it also came to me that there is only
one gospel for all of us, even though it demands differing
responses according to our situation, and that in the ultimate sense the good news to the poor that brings bad
news to the rich is in fact the good news for the rich—not
from their present point of reference but from the gospel's
point of reference.

Was the word of liberation from God for the Israelites
through Moses good news or bad news to Pharaoh? From
Pharaoh's present system of economic and political exploitation, it was strictly bad news. And let us not naively
interpret this as though it were not a political and economic
issue with a theological grounding. But from the standpoint
of the gospel, it was strictly good news, offering to free the
Israelites from their bondage and to free Pharaoh from his
bondage of basing his life on oppression. For Pharaoh the
call of God through Moses is liberation of his life for justice,
for a new humanity, for a new ambition of shared community. Likewise John Newton discovered that the gospel
sounded like bad news before he experienced it as good
news, amazing grace for slave traders.

Liberation theologies are God's way of loving some of
us enough to disturb us. The blessed disturbance comes
with a blessed assurance that in connecting with the under-
privileged or so-called least of these in new structures of
justice and human dignity, we fulfill our true purpose and
meaning in life. The fact is, the good news frequently
sounds like bad news until we journey toward the mind and
love of Christ. Did not the Gerasene demoniac beseech

Jesus not to disturb his demons to which he had become accustomed? And did not the disturbance become a healing which brought him into his right mind, his true self? And did this incredible change not scare the living daylights out of the whole neighborhood? To the point, as we have seen, that they begged Jesus to depart and take his healing disturbance to the next town?

Letty Russell reminds us that the gospel disorients us in order to reorient us.[14] Robert McAfee Brown insists that Jesus Christ dislocates us in order to relocate us.[15] In order to be restored, we must be restoried—restoried in the archetypal images and truths of Abraham and Sarah, Jacob and Rebecca, Shiprah and Puah, Isaiah and Jeremiah, Mary and Mary Magdalene, and the One who is the Champion of the World's Untouchables. This vision of God's disturbing and liberating grace, recalling the church to its foundations in the One who announced and acted in love for the lepers, the hemorrhaging woman, the outcasts, can lead us as clerical and lay leaders in the church to examine our Camelot from the perspective of God's Covenant.

Liberation theologies are not occasional novelties that we try on for size or intriguing sermon topics for Lent soon to be forgotten. Rather, they constitute a framework for ministry, a way of listening, a way of learning, a framework from which we live out the faith. If it is true that liberation theologies offer a deepening relationship with Jesus Christ through justice and shalom for a wider segment of humanity, then we can view such theologies as both gift and challenge to all of us.

Gifts and Challenges for the People of God

Insofar as we look at life and history from the standpoint of the gospel, liberation theologies offer us a whole spectrum of gifts and challenges. From where many of us have stood, indeed, stand even today, the gifts may have a bittersweet flavor which we are not sure we want, and the challenges may seem more like threats or intimidations. Be that as it may, from the standpoint of the gospel they *are* gifts and challenges for our own freedom and sanctification. Theologies from ethnic, feminist, and Third World perspectives have helped me to see more clearly the distance between my Camelot and God's Covenant and Rule.

Consider these: the gift and challenge of less human suffering and wider human options for personal fulfillment and service to others; the gift and challenge of a greater appreciation and recognition of inclusiveness of all people as the children of God; an expanded hermeneutic or interpretive base for the Bible, so that we are freed from narrow cultural contexts for a richer application; a greater approximation of justice, the doing away with double standards of law and customs, and the corresponding strengthening of human dignity and freedom; the uncovering of a greater array of men and women of faith throughout the history of biblical faith, thus enriching our Christian heritage; the shattering of cultural stereotypes to encourage greater utilization of God-given talents and the lessening of debased self-images fostered by the dominant culture; a more global perspective enlarging our concept of God; the changing of systems and structures which favor the powerful while dehumanizing others. Surely we will be found wanting if these possibilities in human history do not matter to us, and if we do not lift up and encourage these directions in our preaching as intrinsic to the gospel.

If our identity is in Jesus Christ—if Jesus Christ is in fact our wisdom, our righteousness, and sanctification and redemption as Paul asserts in 1 Cor. 1—we are free from rationalizing and paralyzing guilt. In Jesus Christ we have nothing to hide and nothing to defend, least of all our own so-called righteousness. If Christ is our righteousness, we need not be defensive about our own performance, our own groups, or any particular way of doing things, even if we have done it that way for years and regardless of what label it carries. When Jesus Christ is the core of our identity, we are free to welcome the human gifts of all persons and groups as contributive to total human well-being instead of as threats to our security and status. Or even if they are threatening to our present way of thinking and being, Jesus

Christ can liberate us from our fear of the success of others and free us for victory in vulnerability.

To North America with Love

Firsthand experience in Latin America has confirmed for me the above assertions on the gifts and challenges of liberation theology. Conversations (with the aid of interpreters) were held with a wide variety of persons and groups in El Salvador and Nicaragua in February 1988. Our group of ecumenical lay and clerical persons, sponsored by the Center for Global Education in Minneapolis, heard from many eyewitnesses and personal sources of the brutality and oppression by the Salvadoran military; we saw the extreme poverty made worse by U.S.-backed war and embargo in Nicaragua; we experienced the incredible courage and hope of base Christian communities and repopulation centers.

Our group exhausted notebooks and pens taking notes from many sessions of listening and inquiry. At one session in Matagalpa, Nicaragua, we were sitting on three benches in a row in a small office, taking notes and trying to understand agrarian reform. The image of "back to school" stuck in my mind. It is not a bad image for North Americans in relation to Latin America. It is not a bad image for preachers who are willing to receive exposure to the lives of the world's majority in whatever way God might bring that to us.

One of our most memorable experiences was a trip several hours from San Salvador to the Santa Marta repopulation community. Over a thousand people had returned from the Mesa Grande refugee camp in Honduras to the site of their previous homes which were destroyed by government ground mortars and air attacks. We saw the remains of their former homes and chapel. This is the result of the ongoing war supported by the United States, a war seldom mentioned in the United States newspapers. The people are rebuilding their homes in the wilderness in the hope that they will not be attacked again. A large white flag thrust in the sky identifies the community as peaceful, with no military arms or guerrillas. We were moved by the one young North American living in solidarity with the community.

Their story is one of immense suffering and tribulation, yet of incredible hope and determination. In a few months they have built sixty homes. No one will move from their present provisional structures to the completed homes across the river until *all* homes are completed and *all* can move together in solidarity. When we asked them the source of their hope, they pointed to two factors: first, the solidarity of their own community in which they experience the presence of Christ; second, visitors from the U.S. whom they implore to impact our government policy in order that we will cease funding the Salvadoran military forces.

In Managua our group worshipped with the Maria de Los Angeles Franciscan congregation. The homily by Fr. Molina was taken from Mark 1:40–45. He pointed out the courage of the leper in coming to Jesus.

> The leper left his hiding place where society had placed him. He broke the Levitical law which required lepers to shout "Unpure, unpure" on all sides. Jesus was faced with the decision whether or not to put himself on the side of the "marginalized." He opted against the priestly caste, and in cleansing the leper Jesus himself became "marginated" forever. Jesus turned all the categories of his time upside down. This is the drama that our people live. The time is past when the gospel is understood strictly within the sacristy. In these forty days of Lent we must follow Jesus. When we enjoin our faith with liberation, we come out of the past. (Notes taken virtually verbatim through translation.)

Many North Americans returning from journeys to Central America often share a similar experience: the people gave us much more than we could give them; . . . they showed us strength beyond human capacity; . . . in their poverty they hosted us and gave to us from their lean store of food; . . . their solidarity speaks for itself and causes us to question the rank individualism of our own life and faith; . . . I learned the true meaning of being "born again."

As for me, I returned with a new sense of apostolic compulsion to speak out on behalf of the people and to review the priorities of my own faith, practice, and preaching. The God of the Covenant and the Kingdom is indeed at work to redefine our various Camelots.

Not everyone can travel to Central America and not everyone draws the same conclusions or is grasped by the same convictions. I do treasure for all of us who preach, however, experiences that are transcultural, multi-social, and polychromatic and polyphonic in color and sound. It is easy to go blind and become deaf to the gospel even when we preach every seven days.

I plan to keep asking myself: Am I free to preach the gospel?

So far our journey together in this book has considered theological content and hermeneutical issues on behalf of preaching with a social conscience. It is time now in chapters 3 and 4 to explore the process and method in this preaching journey.

Chapter Three

Preaching for Holistic Transformation

He had begun his ministry with an understanding of
Christian preaching as "evangelism and the doctrine of
Christian influence," but had advanced to a larger conviction: ". . . that the Christian must do battle for what was
right, and that right was inextricably bound up with
public affairs."[1]

The other tendency to which good preaching is opposed
is a kind of subjectivity that assumes we are free or able
to conjure up private worlds that may exist in a domesticated sphere without accountability to or impingement
from the larger public world. Such a powerful deception
among us seems to offer happiness, but it is essentially
abdication from the great public issues that shape our
humanness.[2]

The first statement reflects on the preaching ministry of
Matthew Simpson, a venerated nineteenth-century Methodist
Episcopal preacher, educator, editor, bishop, and friend of
Abraham Lincoln, who became a forerunner of a series of
Methodist preachers to the nation at large. The second
statement is from biblical scholar Walter Brueggemann.
Together these insights introduce the theme of this chapter.

Naming this chapter was something of a wrestling
match. A number of candidates made their case. Call me
Preaching on Social Issues, one insisted. A member of the
same family requested Preaching on Controversial Issues
(the name of a 1953 book by Harold Bosley). Yet another
contestant clamored for Preaching for Social Transformation, and still another, Preaching for Social Evangelization.

Preaching for Justice also demanded consideration. All of these are well in the ball park. When you read this chapter you will name it as you see fit. In the meantime it will be labeled as indicated above. Even though the term *holistic* may be overused with a tinge of trendiness, it assists in communicating the intent and the content of the chapter.

The gospel, both in its pastoral and in its prophetic voice, insists on a *holistic* hope even when our initial concern seems to be social in nature. This notion has been confirmed in some exciting ways in seminary preaching class. A particular class for which I have responsibility centers on preaching related to public affairs and social concerns. What we have experienced is a growing awareness of our varied neighbors constituting the human face of "issues." Beginning with the notion of prophetic preaching on controversial issues we inevitably are drawn into the pastoral concern for the life situation of human beings. Some of our invisible neighbors have become more visible in our consciousness—people with AIDS, refugees, abused women and children (and sometimes men), the hungry and homeless, the economic underclass, to name a few. The feedback in preaching class is that homiletical homework has become a means of a deeper vision into humanity as well as how preaching might address the variety of human conditions from the standpoint of the gospel. We cannot settle for either individual or social transformation.

The Prophetic Instinct

In spite of the fact that the Old Testament prophets did not have the responsibility for the ongoing ministry of the Word, Sacrament, and Order in congregational life, there is much in their varied ministries that speaks to both clergy and laity in today's church. Even though the setting for preaching today bears little outer resemblance to the times of Jeremiah or Hosea, and even though our culture is different in surface appearance, the need for a prophetic word is as urgent today as in the eighth century B.C. Even though the Hebrew Prophets were frequently regarded as the troublemakers of Israel, in fact they sought to *conserve* the deepest truths of the religious tradition through their future visioning and social criticism. The Prophets drew on the Torah (Hosea 4), from Exodus (Amos 9), and from the Genesis narratives (Hosea 12), to cite several examples.

In the prophetic tradition preachers today are called to discern the activity of God in corporate life and public affairs; we are called to proclaim a Word-embracing social justice and concern for the oppressed; at times we must bring God's judgment on our nation and on the church, a judgment which challenges the ease of Zion and Camelot and offers a redeemed future.[3]

Given our Judeo-Christian tradition we can do no less than keep the entire range of human life within the judging love of God. One of our first presuppositions in preaching is that there is no issue or concern that is beyond the bounds of Christian preaching. To say otherwise is to proclaim the death or irrelevance of God in some particular dimension of life. Harold Bosley, pastor of First Methodist Church in Evanston in the 1950s, liked to say that all vital issues are controversial and that therefore the only way to avoid controversial issues is to avoid vital issues. We can explain honest mistakes but can we explain silence?

Prophetic ministry is too often identified solely with spasms of protest. Prophetic ministry does not necessarily imply spectacular social crusading or abrasive measures of indignation. If I read the Scripture correctly, the prophetic instinct is normative for *all* our ministry. The prophetic instinct is a way of life and ministry seeking to be faithful to the whole gospel. Witness to justice is not optional for the body of Christ, rather such concern and action is inevitably prophetic as it brings judgment on injustice. Peacemaking is not optional for the community of faith, yet its serious quest is bound to be controversial with those who benefit from militarism. Hospitality to sojourners in our land is a gospel imperative in response to God's compassionate love, but it is sometimes in direct conflict with deportation policies and practices of the Immigration and Naturalization Service of our government. "To think of the church as being inherently prophetic rather than simply

having a prophetic task makes its profoundest impact on
how the church is present."[4]

A Reflection of Our Total Ministry

Preaching which attempts to connect the gospel with
the whole fabric of the human condition should be no
surprise to those whom we represent in Christ. The purpose
of our preaching is not at odds with leading corporate
worship, counseling with George and Sally, teaching the
Susannah Bible Class, or serving on the board of the local
juvenile detention center.

As representatives of the faith community our whole
ministry should be a testimony to concern for all kinds of
people and issues. If our ministry is close to Jesus Christ,
we will be seen and heard in many settings as those who
exemplify God's love for all persons, and for systems that
honor dignity and human worth. Peace with justice is not
to be a sudden, jarring slogan from the pulpit; it should
characterize our whole ministry. What should seem odd to
parishioners is our silence from the pulpit on major questions of the day, a silence inconsistent with the rest of our
ministry.

Preaching with a Prophetic Instinct

Prophetic preaching is a contextual interpretation of
God's Word based on the belief that God loves us enough
to disturb us.[5] The gospel is not only "Blessed Assurance,
Jesus is Mine," but also "Blessed Disturbance, We are
Christ's!" Indeed, the biblical narratives as a whole have to
do with God moving in on the human scene contradicting
the way things are.

The late Rabbi Abraham Heschel described the function of the prophets as one of *interference*. The Scripture is in fact a story of loving interference and inquiry, bringing inconvenience in order to heal and hallow life—burning bushes, whirlwinds, pillars of fire, holy of holies, the still small voice, prophetic woes, and "you have heard it said . . . but I tell you." Only because God loves us enough to inquire, to invade, to disturb us, is there transforming power in the gospel.

The genius of biblical tradition unites judgment and mercy on behalf of a healing wholeness. God's love is a disturbing influence and power; God's judgment is a renewing and re-creating catharsis. Critical love in the biblical sense is neither agreement nor rejection. It rescues from illusion and idolatry, pointing to a new future. For this reason we must encourage the faith community to *expect* a biblically and theologically informed disturbance as a dimension of the redemptive Word. Otherwise the ethos of the Christian church inevitably begins to sound introverted and all too fallibly human, and thereby loses its authority to change life.

The context for prophetic preaching is a theology that embraces all of life. If a congregation has a growing appreciation for the inclusiveness of Christian faith, then prophetic preaching will not seem an intrusion into so-called secular matters nor an abandonment of the biblical and historic gospel. I use the term prophetic preaching in the broad, general sense of a message that attempts to interpret the Word or will of God in a way that cuts across prevailing norms and practices.

Whether we are neophytes in the pulpit or seasoned preachers desiring to explore a deeper dimension for our preaching, there are some "user friendly" ground rules to consider on behalf of preaching for holistic transformation. Here are some that have taught me over the years. I commend them for your reflection and conversation.

Ground Rules of Preaching for Holistic Transformation

a) Personal Motivation

The prophetic instinct calls for careful reflection on our motivation for preaching focused on social concerns and issues. What are our prejudices? Are we prepared to speak the truth, as we understand it, in love? Are we preaching in anger in a way that will lay guilt trips on our listeners, or is there a spirit of sorrow and lamentation undergirding our concerns, as so often reflected, for example, in Jeremiah? Are we more interested in portraying ourselves as champions of the "marginalized" or is there a deep and abiding conviction about the gospel's relevance to people who hurt, including those in our own congregation?

During the Vietnam War, I was visited with one of the most powerful dreams of my life. It came as a revelation. At the time I was a pastor in Dallas taking a strong and visible stand in and out of the pulpit against the war. In the dream I was on a cobblestone street in some far away country, perhaps in Eastern Europe. Along came—in living color—a whole convoy of army trucks. Standing in the backs of the trucks were crammed groups of grizzled old war veterans with chests full of clanging medals. As they passed by I felt hatred for them in a way that to this day brings an emotional response of remorse in recalling the dream.

Upon awaking the dream was crystal clear, even as it is today after more than twenty years. The dream had a clear message: I had allowed my protest of a system to become indistinguishable from detesting individuals connected with the system. Persons in the military had become my "nigger" and I had condemned them as human beings. No one could ever convince me that this dream was anything other than a word from God, bringing the disturbing, healing grace that reconciles and transforms. The nocturnal wrestling match did not change my position on the war. It did radically alter my level of compassion for individuals caught up in massive systems and the level of discernment as to the individuality of persons within those systems. The road from Camelot to Covenant is not paved with self-righteousness or a sense of moral superiority.

In the appendix of *Preaching as a Social Act*, Arthur Van Seters poses a set of critically important questions for preachers to consider. Under the heading "Personal Socialization of the Preacher," he asks:

> What in my own life journey is influencing me in the preparation and delivery of this sermon? How has my socialization influenced the way I involve (or am reluctant to involve) the congregation/parish in the preaching process? How has my socialization shaped my views about preaching on social and political issues?[6]

b) Purpose

I have found it important to ask myself "What am I 'after'" in the sermon which attempts to relate the gospel to Salvadoran refugees? This will frequently be a secondary question of purpose since the primary one will be "What is the text after? What does it say? Where does it lead us?" When we have wrestled with these questions, we will be grasped by a number of possibilities, regardless of whether our beginning place is text or topic.

A sermon can serve the purpose of confirming and validating hidden courage in the heart of the listeners. We could call it a "naming" or "moment of recognition" in which the congregant will say to him- or herself, "I'm right after all to believe that Christians should reach out to people suffering from AIDS." Or that the pulse of the gospel calls for more attention to health and education in the public domain and less expenditure of resources for military hardware. Thus the homiletical form of prophetic instinct can affirm a life-giving ethos which undergirds our value orientation and decision making.

The prophetic imagination in preaching can also encourage the listener to test his or her presuppositions from a biblical and theological base. In a recent seminar exploring liberation theologies I asked the lay participants to identify the resources by which their view of liberation theology had been formed. Without exception they named various television newscasts about Latin America, *Time*, *Wall Street Journal*, *U.S. News and World Report* and similar journals. It was not surprising that for the most part their opinions were on a range between neutral to negative. None had read any original sources from a theologian nor heard in person anyone representing liberation theology. We have few greater challenges than to strengthen the biblical and theological foundation of the congregation so that our perspectives are informed by these foundations which undergird and guide the faith community.

> . . . preaching about social concerns includes not only guiding people toward specific stances but also giving them the resources to arrive at such stances on their own. It involves helping them build a structure of being from which prophetic understandings of issues will naturally flow.[7]

Challenge and call to decision are the informing motivations behind some of our sermons with prophetic intent. Our purpose may be a challenge to give up certain presuppositions or positions, though in the final analysis our Christian faith sinks or swims not by our negations but by our life-giving affirmations. As a church and as human beings we cannot live faithfully merely by what we are against but by our positive commitments and actions. To rail against the excesses of consumer-oriented Camelots is futile. To point with passion to the depth of life in the Covenant is a message of hope and transformation. "We reprove best when we share vision, raise sights, open horizons."[8]

A hopeful vision is thus another goal of prophetic preaching. The Christian pulpit stands in the time-honored tradition of an Ezekiel who discerns the activity of God in giving life to the dry bones of Israel; or an Isaiah who meets the despair of a people in exile with a prophecy of faith, hope, and expectancy, and a later Isaiah through whom God authorizes a radical reinterpretation of the fast from sackcloth and ashes to an ethical act of compassion and justice. In Israel the future in God's freedom is usually not without call to repentance but it offers the most profound hope. It is no different in our time.

c) Pastoral Sensitivity

Anyone who has served for any length of time in a pastorate can hardly fail to notice the close connection between the pastoral and the prophetic. Effective preaching always involves a relationship of trust between preacher and people, and doubly so when it comes to prophetic preaching. If we have moved *toward* people faithfully as a shepherd, they may also allow us to move toward them as prophets from whom they have already experienced care and concern. Lee S. Moorehead writes: "Since preaching is an audacious and almost arrogant business, we who engage in it ought to realize that we cannot be tolerated unless we speak out of lives of humble service."[9]

The pastoral and the prophetic belong together not only in the functioning of the ordained, but also in the Covenant faith and life of the people of God. The prophetic ministry is not an elitist possession of the ordained, but the very meaning of being called into the Covenant. To be called is to be sent, and it is for this reason that prophetic preaching and ministry are the function of *both* clergy and laity in relation to the world.

During most of my fifteen-year ministry in the local pastorate I took the freedom of the pulpit more or less for granted. I did not lack awareness of its importance nor did I ever knowingly exploit it. But looking back, I can now appreciate more deeply the potential contribution of mutual explorations with the laity on our expectations for freedom of the pulpit.

What does freedom of the pulpit mean to the preacher? to the people? What are its limits? What are the responsibilities of both clergy and laity? The issue of prophetic preaching is inevitably linked with a theology of the pulpit, and I can only suggest here that it could be worthwhile for the preacher and the congregation to explore these questions together. Done carefully, it could pave the way for a mutual set of expectations for preaching, and especially for attempts at prophetic utterances.

The pulpit should be one means among several to address key issues of our time. During my pastorates I discovered later than I should have that controversial preaching topics could also be explored in symposiums and dialogues involving the laity in firsthand discussion. In September 1967, following months of soul-searching and research, I offered two sermons opposing the Vietnam War in affirmation of a peaceful vision and hope. The sermons attempted a "speaking the truth in love" style but at the same time carried a "thus saith the Lord" conviction.

The sermons evoked both appreciation and conflict— and some loss of membership. It became apparent that we needed an opportunity for members of the congregation to face one another, as well as the pastor, on the issue. Soon we held an evening session with a panel featuring various positions on the war. This opportunity could have been connected with the original sermon—that is, a simultaneous doubleheader involving the preached Word in the morning, followed that evening by an opportunity for all viewpoints to be expressed. Or one could make a case for public airing first, then the preaching event. The more controversial a topic, the more there is need to consider a forum for hearing different opinions.

Today's rightful emphasis on consultation, collegiality, and democratic participation must not obscure the responsibility of the pulpit to relate the gospel to all of life. *Freedom of the pulpit* is not subject to the balloting of prevailing opinion. But we preachers should be aware that our more or less captive audience in the pews is composed of colleagues in the faith, and that there is a time and a place for mutual sharing. A *sensitive minister* will recognize that truth is often served by the shared insights and experiences of the faith community, to say nothing of the right of people to express themselves and to be heard.

d) Confessional, Vulnerable Style

Through the years I have tried to learn about and understand various styles in prophetic sermons. Instead of what could loosely be called the "Amos style" of confrontation and accusation, I have come to appreciate more deeply the wisdom and efficacy of an *inquiring* mode of prophetic preaching which seeks to pierce heart and soul with the penetrating question. There is a time for parable and poetry which are not perfectly clear cut but which touch and tease some hidden archetypal nerve, like the playful and haunting melody of a heavenly flute.

The God-human encounter in Scripture focuses on combinations of the *indicative* and the *imperative*. The shape of the gospel at times is a form of the indicative, which represents proclamation, pronouncement, assertion: in the beginning God created; God is love; the reign of God is at hand. The imperative mode of divine-human confrontation is frequently a command or exhortation: follow me; go into the world; love your enemies. This mode is the call to action of much of the biblical narratives.

As biblical scholars have shown, the indicative, imperative, and interrogative are expressed in a variety of ways, and especially in Paul's writing they have the closest connection—indeed, are inclusive of one another. Indicative statements may be used to exhort, thus carrying imperative force, just as questions may have an essentially imperative thrust.

I believe it is the questioning, inquiring style that has great promise in some of our prophetic preaching. The interrogative mode may be simply another form of the indicative or the imperative, but it reaches out to the listener in a different way. The inquiring approach lends itself to a confessional style and a mutual search rather than dogmatic coercion. Thus there is less likelihood of misusing biblical texts than otherwise might be the case.

In Scripture God is the Ultimate Questioner of all our questions and all our answers. As Gerhard Ebeling put it in *The Nature of Faith*, when we speak of God, we are speaking of the "radical question about where man is, the question which concerns him unconditionally."[10] In the teachings of Jesus, more than 150 questions are addressed to his disciples: what does it profit you to gain the whole world . . . ? Why do you see the speck . . . ? Which of you by being anxious . . . ? False prophets, ancient and contemporary, offer simple answers and an ecclesiastical happy-hour as a substitute for worshipping the Holy One of Israel. Prophets of God raise penetrating and disturbing questions.

The inquiring style is conducive to growth for both preacher and listener. It appeals to imagining and to searching more deeply. And it suggests that even in the name of God we preachers are frequently uncertain and befuddled like everyone else. We all know that there are countless problems in our time of history which are neither present nor envisioned in any direct sense in biblical times—nuclear energy, genetic engineering, and environmental complexities arising from modern technology. We may not know the answers to many of society's social ills and injustices, but we had better know the questions which lead us and even drive us to watching and waiting in expectant ways for God's prompting toward greater clarity and certainty.

I urge seminary students not to be afraid to reveal some personal faith struggle in their sermons. It needs to be clear to both pulpit and pew that the gospel addresses the preacher no less than the congregation. I have often found myself saying something like, "This is a difficult word for all of us to hear, and believe me, it's not easy to speak it either. It's one of those sayings that I sometimes wish Jesus had never said or that the early church had neglected to preserve, but here it is, as I came to it through my own faith and biblical study. . . ."

Our preaching seeks to be beyond dogmatism yet also beyond majority vote, to be more than personal opinion by the grace of the Holy Spirit yet less than the hot air of presumptuous infallibility. A lay person once said of her preacher: "She preaches with conviction and passion but she never backs me into a corner as though to disagree with her position is automatically to be against God. She leaves you room to wiggle." That is what we are aiming for as preachers of the Word!

The confessional posture helps our listeners to hear because there is human credibility behind the pulpit. It leads to a realization that the preacher is one of us, representing us, even though set apart for this difficult but essential responsibility of being God's messenger of the Word.

e) Biblical Foundation

There is a sense in which *none* of the biblical texts are directed toward the corporate ills of today's world and a sense in which *all* of the texts bear possible application. The twentieth century is vastly different in world view from the time when texts were formed and preserved. More important is the eschatological factor which permeates the New Testament. An ongoing world and church with a mission in some future century is simply not part of the immediate framework of the biblical texts.

On the other hand all the texts are "community" texts, shaped and preserved by the faith community. They are not addressed as privileged messages for isolated individuals in Camelots of their own devising as seems to be the assumption of much verbiage passed off as Christianity in present-day North America. The considerable variety of texts formed and transmitted verbally and eventually canonized in written form *by the community* point to a Covenant relationship between God and the faith community. In this indirect sense all texts bear potential significance in relation to the purpose of God in creating and sustaining community locally, nationally, and across the globe.

In a more specific sense there are several ways we can approach preaching for the holistic transformation inherent in the Covenant. I will lift up three for our purposes.

First, all texts should be considered sensitively and imaginatively from the standpoint of prophetic, Covenant-oriented instinct. By remembering the community origin and context of the biblical passage, then recalling that the faith community— the body of Christ, the people of God—exists only for the wider community as a sign of the Rule of God, our preaching will reflect this biblical posture.

The constant gravitational pull of congregational life is toward a "Camelot Club House" serving its own needs in lieu of others'. This is as true of the congregation as it is of our personal lives. The reason God has placed the congregation in its particular location is to serve the people that live in the community and beyond. The relationship to the immediate community, whether rural or urban, and to society in larger perspective determines to what degree you have a church of the Covenant and/or of a comfortable, introverted Camelot. The content of the preaching shapes and directs the choice.

I am suggesting that preaching from Camelot to Covenant does not depend on selecting a text with more or less obvious relevance to social concerns or issues, but to show that every text is relevant to social concerns. Show how the lament of the lonely Psalmist connects with lonely and isolated people today. Make connections between God's unconditional love and our basic attitudes toward those we are inclined to label and treat as enemies. Take the seemingly innocuous "do this in remembrance of me" and suggest the global consciousness inherent in the act of eucharistic sharing.

Preaching from the lectionary can be alert and empathic to justice and peace themes of the Christian year. A genuinely helpful resource for the Camelot-to-Covenant preaching journey is entitled *Social Themes of the Christian Year, A Commentary on the Lectionary*, edited by Dieter T. Hessel.[11] Utilizing a liberation hermeneutic, the several authors provide essays and articles for social-ethical Scripture interpretation for the three-year cycle of the Christian year. Socially significant theological themes of the various seasons are identified and interpreted. The authors describe their method of biblical interpretation as critically conscious, canonically informed, christologically based, contextually shaped, and communally developed. "We highlight a liberating social hermeneutic that features ethics and praxis in its discipline of biblical interpretation."[12]

Their method is further described:

> Liberating theological reflection begins with prophetic imagination or alternative consciousness (Brueggemann)—which questions the dominant world view and criticizes the status quo because it is hopeful for a better future. The active community of faith brings to its interpretation of biblical texts an expectation of God's transforming action and an "exegetical suspicion" that important human social realities have been overlooked in prevailing interpretations of the Bible. "Liberated hermeneutics is the decision to look at all Scripture first

against the backdrop of despair, deprivation, and exploitation which characterizes the circumstances of most humanity and to ask what God's word says about that reality" (Owensby).[13]

The biblical text, whether lectionary or chosen by the preacher, may thus suggest an indirect leading into a concern of even several connections which will be part of the sermon movement but not necessarily the main theme or thrust.

In chapter 2 we considered the pericope in Matthew 9:32–34 in which Jesus casts out a demon from a man unable to speak, thus calling forth voice amid silence. Verses 18–34 of the same chapter taken as a whole bring us a whole series of healings. It is enough to make your head swim. I like to call it the "Hill Street Blues" text. They are all there—the powerful, the marginal, the invisible, the outcast. It is a pretty fair representation of our churches and of society both national and global. I originally preached on vss. 18–26 on the anniversary of Martin Luther King's birthday. I called my sermon "When the Funeral Music Has Already Begun." Part of it sounded like this:

> The text tells us that while he is yet speaking, Jesus receives an emergency call in person. A ruler—Mark's version identifies him as Jairus, a synagogue official—implores Jesus to come and restore life to his daughter. So Jesus responds to the crisis. When he arrives at the ruler's home, he encounters flute players and a tumultuous crowd. The Talmud says that even the poor were expected to provide two flute players and one wailing woman. In short, *the funeral music has already begun.* In other words, the ritual of death is already under way. Expectations are set, realities have been named, the dice have been thrown and counted by the house, the score is clear. . . .

> We're told that Jesus *calls forth life amid the conditions of death.* The process of death is reversed and life is restored. Life restored is no guarantee, but a gift. Life restored is not simply a long-ago, magic-like power known only to Jesus, nor is life restored simply a matter of having enough faith and curing ourselves. Life restored—*in* every age and *at* every age—is a mysterious collaboration and convergence of God's presence and power and the

human response of faith and hope. Not one without the other, but both. Sometimes this happens dramatically and suddenly, but usually it happens over a period of time.
. . .

When Martin Luther King arrived on the scene in the footsteps of this text, the funeral music had been playing for a long time—ever since the days of slavery, to be exact. In the midst of death's ritual he called forth a whole nation from the death of racism and injustice to the life of freedom and respect for self and others. Today's celebration, then, is a thanksgiving for progress made and a challenge for progress to come. King's legacy is one of courage and hope, a testimony that the sounds of death may well be harbingers of life restored.

Using the text's thrust of Jesus' calling forth life amid the conditions of death, I related the text to a nurturing, stabilizing interpretation and then to societal issues today. The nurturing connection centered around the story of a local woman who operated a shelter for troubled teenagers. "If there's anything worth saving," she said, "I want to do it." The societal direction raised questions about factors in our society which result in death and those that are life-affirming. Can we as a nation be the world's leading seller of arms and at the same time expect our citizens to use nonviolent means to solve social ills? Can we as a church be a sign of hope for the hungry and homeless in our society?

Another example in the same chapter suggests relating the healing of the woman with a hemorrhage in Matt. 9:18–26 to the chronic bleeding in our society today in the form of the feminization of poverty. How might the church be touched by this condition and how might we redemptively respond? How might we hear Jesus Christ calling forth wholeness amid the conditions of sickness? Our intent in the sermon may be awareness of suffering of others, or a call to activate the imagination and confession of the congregation in developing a response.

A second approach for Camelot-to-Covenant preaching is the use of a text which suggests a more direct, specific application related to one issue. Again, the text may come from the lectionary or be the preacher's choice. "Blessed are the peacemakers, for they shall be called sons of God" (Matt. 5:9). This verse from the Sermon on the Mount could be the centerpiece for a sermon or even a series on Christians as peacemakers. We would want to begin with the context and with Matthew's purpose and proceed to search out those ways in which the Christian community is by definition meant to be a sign of peace. Other texts could be the controlling factor in sermons calling forth justice (Isa. 58:3–12), stewardship of the earth (from Gen. 1), compassion for the sojourner (Deut. 10:12–22), the risk of being a neighbor (Luke 10:25–37). In each instance, the preacher is to let the text tell its contextual story and only then to probe its "gospel" for today.

Faithful expository preaching and use of the lectionary as a foundation for preaching have characterized homiletical literature in the past decade as well as my own approach to biblical grounding in this section. Even so we need not rule out *a third approach, namely, responsible topical preaching which addresses the concerns of the Covenant.* There is no prohibition ruling out the searching of a text as resource for that particular sermon by a preacher with deep human concerns illuminated by biblical roots.[14]

I do not recommend it as a regular preaching method for the reason that it courts the undesirable problem of placing the Scripture in an ongoing secondary position to the preacher's ideas and priorities, even where these are profoundly humane and supported by the gospel. But it has its place, especially in response to major community events, special community needs, and national catastrophes. Who wants to insist on automatically preaching from the lectionary following the president's assassination or the space shuttle disaster?

f) Theological Examination

Through the years I have learned to ask myself a number of theological questions that seem critical for faithful Covenant preaching, questions which the gospel asks you and me. In previous chapters we have already reflected on the matter of continuing to wrestle with the factors that

shape our basic theological presuppositions and the result-
ing effect on our preaching. Here I want to lift up very
briefly three theological inquiries which I direct to myself
and recommend for others.

First, what is God doing in the sermon text and how
does that relate to what we perceive God doing in the world
today? This question leads me to speak theocentrically or
christologically as appropriate for the foundation of the
sermon. To do so is always basic, yet it is even more important to the listener in sermons grappling with difficult
public matters. Obviously, this does not guarantee faithfulness to either text or gospel. Just as it is easier to preach
the Bible unbiblically than biblically,[15] so theological language can be used untheologically. Yet if our opening questions can connect the human situation with what God has
done and is doing, we may be on the right track. The right
track includes divine action in perspective rather than our
own pat answers to social ills and an imperative informed
and grounded in the indicative.

A closely related second question is, "Am I speaking
theologically rather than ideologically?" Sometimes there
is a fine line between calling for public policy in the pulpit
and bringing a dimension of the gospel to bear on the ethos
or value system undergirding certain policies and practices.
I recall William Sloane Coffin's comment related to the fifth
chapter of Amos, namely, that our task as preachers is to
call forth justice and righteousness like an overflowing
stream, not to construct the irrigation ditches. We have
clear biblical mandates to condemn starvation, exploitation, and dehumanization. Furthermore, it is possible to be
quite specific concerning causes as well as consequences,
assuming we have done our "homework."

We can and must point to those values and hopes that
are consistent with the Reign of God. For example, in the
name of the gospel the pulpit may challenge the nuclear
arms build-up, the lack of serious effort to negotiate disar-
mament, and a governmental stance that favors the affluent
and increases the misery of the disadvantaged. In the name
of God we raise the humane question, challenge the moral
ethos from a biblical and theological grounding, lift up

those values that appear to be consistent with the mind of Christ, and point to the judgment and love of God present in every situation.

However, it is more difficult and more questionable to identify the gospel or a Christian solution with a particular political or economic program lest we legitimate ideological stances. We must be painstakingly careful about assuming the position of policymakers or suggesting that we possess the "how to" expertise when it comes to restructuring society. As Peter Berger has observed, "The idea that moral sensitivity somehow bestows the competence to make policy recommendations . . . is delusional."[16] Our biblical foundation is more conducive to lifting up the purposes and priorities of the Reign of God or of the mind of Christ than to detailing specifics of programs and policies. What is essential is to portray clearly the human situation or predicament in the perspective of God's Word.

A third question on the way from Camelot to Covenant is, "Do the sermon's notions of sin and grace seem to come from the text in a way appropriate for the congregation, and do the notions deserve each other?" All that can be suggested here is an indication of the type of concern I have in mind. Is the theology of the human condition in the sermon centered in pride and will-to-power or in self-abnegation and dependence on others for one's self-definition? Is the theology of grace directed at a hubris pretending to be more than we were created to be or at a self-abasement content to be less than we were meant to be in God? How do these choices relate to the text and to this congregation? These questions and others like them need continual testing and assessment in our sermon preparation.

g) Secular Research

Preaching on social issues requires careful research, especially if an entire sermon is so engaged. Some issues appear to be relatively clear and unambiguous whereas others seem to be much more complicated and perplexing. Of course, just as beauty is in the eye of the beholder

(Margaret Wolfe Hungerford), so the relevance of the
gospel to a particular issue varies from person to person.

Even the denouncing or calling into question of specific
evils will likely require careful examination. Of course,
some forms of oppression are so blatant that this is less the
case. Frequently, however, we have to choose between two
or more undesirable possibilities. If a large corporation
employing thousands of people is polluting a lake with
waste by-products, for example, we might have to choose
between a devastated environment or the loss of jobs for
hundreds of families, with the accompanying social consequences. Having come into the ordained ministry from a
business perspective, I have long been convinced that one
of the worst habits of some prophetic preaching is the
naiveté and lack of good hard research undergirding the
attempt.

There will always be an element of ambiguity in any
complex social issue—if not in relation to ends, then to
means, and not infrequently in connection with consequences themselves. Irreducible ambiguity should not retard our
willingness to speak out from the pulpit, but we owe it to
our calling and to the church to be as well informed as
possible. The facts, insofar as we can ascertain them, are
never all "in," but we should proceed on as solidly factual
a ground as possible before presuming to interpret the
gospel in relation to a specific issue. The credibility of
prophetic preaching depends on trust and caring relationships. It also depends on accuracy of information and
knowledge so that our case is not prejudiced at the outset
owing to ignorance and oversimplification on our part.

Harold Bosley urged preachers to get a clear picture of
the opposite view. The preacher's research, he said, "must
be as careful and as conscientious as that of a lawyer preparing an important brief or a surgeon preparing to deal with
a delicate and dangerous ailment." [17]

In *Preaching Christian Doctrine* William J. Carl III holds
before the reader a summary of William Sloane Coffin's
threefold pattern "for doctrinal preaching on personal and
global moral problems."[18] The pattern suggests a route
similar to the preceding paragraphs in this chapter outlin-

ing holistic transformation preaching, though in different order:

1. Identify the problem in culture; do homework on it to determine whether it deserves attention in preaching and to understand it fully.

2. Understand the biblical and theological position on the moral problem in question.

3. Bring the religious vision to bear on public life and policy, and do so pastorally.[19]

There is no magic formula for determining the right time or even the right issue for speaking out. My own decision to speak out with a prophetic intention has usually been the culmination of a combination of factors: a growing personal conviction; considerable reflection and soul-searching, including my motivation and the possible objectives of a proposed sermon; an attempt to grasp the fundamental cause-and-effect shape of the issue; an exploration of biblical narratives for clues and connections; and an encounter with persons victimized by a particular injustice.

Often an issue has begun to tug at my heart and mind because of the struggle of a parishioner with this issue, so that it has become *my* issue, and thus *our* issue, in a way not so before that time. The late Reinhold Niebuhr developed his acute social awareness partly because he had to come to grips with the suffering of his parishioners while he was a young pastor in an inner-city area of Detroit. Under this "baptism of fire," he came to see that individual caring and social caring were of the same fabric and that the two could not be separated in the ministry of the church.

An Ancient Journey Ever New

The Reign of God proclaimed by Jesus is forever present and coming. It is God's comprehensive coverage of all people, relationships, and issues. Prayer, piety, principalities, and power are all enfolded and encountered. The gift and claim of God's Reign impacts and impinges on sparrows and systems alike.

Our various preaching traditions at their best have sought to preach an integrated gospel and law that both announced the Rule of God and activated response to that Rule, a preaching journey from the blueprints of our own Camelot to the larger and eternal design of the Covenant.

The whole family of God and the whole company of preachers will do well to hear the testimony to preaching from Archbishop Oscar Romero:

> The church preaches its liberation just as we have studied it today in the Holy Bible—a liberation that has above all, respect for the dignity of the person, the saving of the common good of the people, and a transcendence that looks before all to God, and from God derives its hope and its force.[20]

This is holistic transformation.

Chapter Four

Preaching from Global Consciousness

Preaching is a global work based on a global gift.

> Jesuchristo, Vida del Mundo
> > Jesus Christus, das Leben der Welt
> Jésus Christ, vie du monde
> > Jesus Christ, the Life of the World.[1]

> La vie, don de Dieu
> > La vida, don de Dios
> Leben, ein Geschenk Gottes
> > Life, a gift of God.[2]

The response of North American seminary students who have been exposed to ministry in other cultures is startling. Almost without exception their reflections lay claim to a life-changing experience. More often than not we are told by these "converts" to global consciousness that the experience is irrevocable and thus a learning for a lifetime.[3] They speak of a freeing involvement which challenges narrow views of the church and at the same time demands a global perspective. In short, their Camelot-like assumptions have been challenged and redefined by seeing the Reign of God at work in one or more cultures beyond their own.

Not everyone can experience other cultures in person, especially from the standpoint of involvement in the church's ministry and its intersection with action of God in that society. Thus it becomes a special challenge and opportunity for ordained clergy to seek out those ways in which our own faith can be deepened by global experience and reflection, and then to preach accordingly.

The church has few tasks more important than enlarging the memory, the awareness, and the sense of identification of its members with people and their conditions of life throughout the world. Yet it is tempting for us to neglect a global vision because with broader knowledge and awareness comes the burden of responsibility. Is it not more to our inclination to shut out the world scene or to succumb to numbness after an endless array of disasters and scenes of human suffering on the TV screen?

Let me make my own confession. When I am in my Camelot mode of thinking and acting, I am likely to draw small protective circles around my life. My sense of story shrinks and revolves around me and a few others in my selective circle. Camelot tends to isolate and insulate me in the predominant ethos of individualism.[4] If the meaning of my life can be reduced to my own well-being, or that of my group or state or nation, then a theology based on global perspective is a nuisance at best and downright bad news at worst. However, if the meaning of my life has to do with all other lives on this planet—if there is cosmic and global connection of life with life as in the Reign of God—then a global consciousness becomes essential to my self-understanding.

To become globally conscious is actually to become aware of *what already is*, something like recognizing the law of gravity. Through television our society has become accustomed to thinking globally, even if superficially, on just about every level. What springs to mind at the mention of 'economics' is: Japanese cars; made in Taiwan; trade tariffs, deficits and agreements; transnational corporations; to divest or not to divest in South Africa; or with regard to politics: Shiite Muslims, East-West, North-South, Persian Gulf, Contras. The interrelatedness and interdependence of the global neighborhood has become the common experiential currency of our daily environment. Unless the church wants to become a dinosaur, we must be concerned to grow global Christians and citizens.

Preaching for a global consciousness is a homiletical first cousin of preaching for holistic transformation. Both are concerned about God's liberating and reconciling purpose in creating and sustaining community based on the justice and love of the Rule of God. But before we can preach *for* a global consciousness, we as preachers need to be able to preach *from* a global perspective which nurtures and informs our own faith and thus our preaching foundation.

Global Consciousness: Caveats and Cautions

A global perspective is not to be construed as an escape from the needs on our own doorstep. Sometimes it seems less demanding to relate to needs across the world than the ones next door, especially since matters close at hand may be constantly visible and involve political and social complexities and risks. Local and global concerns should strengthen each other, so that we see more clearly the plight of "marginalized" people in Central America and in our own vicinity. If some parishioners give priority to the local and others to the global, it simply means a variety of gifts utilized in different ways. Talk with each other, learn from each other, and support one another. Ministry does not demand narrow either/or choices by congregations.

On the other hand global consciousness is not intended to take on the whole world and all its problems. This is a second caution. Selectivity of mission is a must and preaching should not suggest otherwise. Unless our global vision is focused, it can overwhelm us, especially if it is not clearly articulated as part of God's creative and redeeming activity.

A global vision is nurtured not only by our concern for others but by the amazing gifts of vision and commitment which people in diverse circumstances have to offer us. The wisdom of those who work among "marginalized" peoples often sounds like "Go to the poor not because they need you but because you need them." The days of paternalism and imperialism are by and large long gone on the global mission scene in which today everyone is both giver and receiver.

Global Consciousness: A Threefold Perspective

By global consciousness I mean a posture, a framework by which we understand our lives in history and by which ministry is imaged and carried out. The Covenant into which God calls us is not a local or regional or national one, but a global gift and claim. God's eternal drama of redemption, reconciliation, and liberation for the whole world is localized in particularity (incarnation, congregation, persons), yet realized within the larger global network of God's action. The part cannot be fully understood or appreciated apart from the whole. A theology of the church's purpose and mission is bound to be defective unless built on a hermeneutic of the global, universal story of the God of history. Anything less than a global consciousness suggests a tribal deity extrapolated from the biases of human consciousness.

In this chapter, I will lift up three basic perspectives as a minimal framework for global consciousness today. These basic areas will provide the roots for the soil of preaching from a global consciousness.

One major perspective is a clear and current view of the Christian world mission. It is no secret that today a major shift in the center of Christian gravity is taking place. The majority of the world's Christians are now people of color, with about fifty-two percent of today's Christians in the Third World. This massive trend reflects the growing strength and influence of what Walbert Buhlmann has called "The Coming of the Third Church" in Africa, Asia, Latin America, and Oceania, as distinguished from Western and Eastern churches. It is estimated that by the year 2000, the beginning of the third Christian millenium, sixty percent of all Christians will live in the Third World.[5]

In his book, *Going Forth: Missionary Consciousness in Third World Catholic Churches*, Omer Degrijse provides an updated view of the coming age of these churches, mostly with regard to the southern hemisphere, and herein summarized:

> – The young churches of the Third World will become the most dynamic wing of the world church, autonomous, responsible, no longer marginal, indigenous, and very much participating in two–way evangelization with churches of North America and Europe;

> – The Roman Catholic Church in Latin America will disassociate itself from the powerful and will make a major turn or shift to the masses of the poor. This will be a model for church renewal, the first church to *reverse* a mistake of centuries . . . so that instead of a moribund, stagnant church of a small minority of the powerful, a church of hope, spiritual richness, and full of youthfulness and growing maturity is emerging;

> – A decade from now we will be confronted with a scenario in which non-Western missionaries will probably outnumber Western missionaries which means a coming end to Western missionary monopoly and a mission liberated from colonial ties and Western cultural embodiment . . . and thus an internationalization of mission personnel, a supranational mission force.[6]

In the closing remarks of his 1985 SMU Ministers' Week Lecture, "God's Mission—Our Ministry," Dr. W. Richey Hogg summarized as follows:

> Let us help our congregations to be alive to the rebirth of Christianity in China, the growth of the church in Korea, the translation of the Scriptures for virtually all peoples, the growing renewal through evangelization in the Roman Catholic Church in Latin America, the witness and dynamic growth—often under persecution—of the faith in Africa, and the emergence of vibrant and challenging theologies from Christians in the Third World.[7]

A second perspective for global consciousness is the significant contribution of various Third World theologies. While a global perspective can by no means be reduced to Third World issues, I do not believe that we can faithfully or effectively grasp or be grasped by a global consciousness in this time of history without taking account of Third World theologies and issues. I have given attention in chapter 2 to the contributions of Third World theologies to

Covenant preaching. It will suffice at this point to reiterate that these theologies lift up the liberating work of God in cultures heretofore defined as marginal by others, thus linking Christians with each other across the globe and frequently with non-Christians on behalf of freedom, justice, and peace.

A third dimension of a global perspective today would surely include the global dialogical engagement among the world's religions. These contacts point to the undeniable fact of global interdependence and the increasing need to understand others and to build bridges of trust and cooperation, especially acting together as allies in our mutual hope and efforts for world peace. Our global perspective will lead us to put ourselves in the shoes of other inhabitants of the earth as best as we can with their help and to remember that only about twenty-five percent of the world's people are Christians by name (about 1.3 billion out of a five billion world population). These figures suggest the urgency for Christians to be in constructive conversation and action with other religions.

So far I have taken a rather wide-angle, three-dimensional lens to offer an overview of basic perspectives of global consciousness. Let us look now with a zoom lens for a narrower focus on two of the gifts and challenges of a global consciousness.

Global Consciousness Enriches, Enlarges, and Enlivens our Concept and Our Experience of God. Kosuke Koyama, a Japanese theologian and author, has spoken of the "center complex" or cultural captivity of deity in Japanese thinking prior to the Second World War. Deity was identified almost solely with national history and tradition. As he put it, "the people didn't realize that God has an international education!"[8]

The tendency to nationalize and tribalize God is seductively present in all countries and has firm roots in biblical times as well. Once a person or a group moves beyond the localization of God to a universal concept, there can be born a renewed sense of purpose, destiny and kinship with all people. Global consciousness leads to wonder and awe of the God of all peoples, the "polychromatic" God who links us together across race, nationality, class, and sex.

In my office at the seminary is a painting by William Zlinak which I call the "Universal Christ Head." It is a head of Christ somehow recognizable as such, yet quite different from other portrayals. The head is made up of countless human faces, some unknown and some recognizable, such as Ghandi. The faces show features of all races and colors, both sexes, children and adults: a global collage. All of humanity is taken up in the form of Christ's head, and yet the Christ is to be recognized in the almost endless variety of human faces. The picture is a mystery that somehow communicates the transcendent incarnation of a universal, all-encompassing Christ in solidarity with humankind.

At Saint Paul School of Theology, where I served from 1973–1985, all first-year students were required to participate in four "-ism" seminars—racism, sexism, classism, and ageism—each being a day and a half in length, spaced at intervals throughout the school year. The rationale is that Christian theology cannot truly be theology in general but only an incarnational theology wrapped around real issues of bondage, oppression, and hope. I began to wonder if a fifth "-ism" seminar was needed, namely, one on parochialism. In our heads at least, if not our systems, the church has moved beyond overt imaging of God in terms of race or age or class. We are now beginning to image God in both male and female metaphorical language. And why not, since both male and female are created in the image of God, and since biblical scholars are in the process of making many corrections from original texts previously translated too narrowly by the gender bias of male scholars. But we continue to image God in only one language, our own.

Now I know you may think this is rather strange, but for me at least, worship is almost literally transformed when another language is utilized. For example, the Scripture—at least one of the lections—is read in Korean, a prayer is given in the Kru dialect of Liberia, or a solo is sung in Spanish. For me the whole service takes on a new dimension, a quality of universality, yet infinite particularity, a sense of the majesty of God, the wonder of cultural differences and a global faith community. With the exception of about a dozen words in German, Spanish, and Japanese, it is the fact that I do *not* understand what is being said that lends an air of mystery, gift, and challenge, a shifting into a transcendent and global gear! The God of history is reflected in all of these languages and faces, yet beyond them all. Beyond ideology, beyond the familiar, beyond me and mine.

I am not suggesting pre-Reformation or pre-Vatican II worship in language alien to the people. As far as I am concerned that battle has been fought and won once and for all. I am suggesting a touch or taste of the international, a reminder of the global God, an enrichment of imagination and image in the life of the church. In other words I believe that *inclusive* language points to *global* inclusiveness as well as *gender* inclusiveness. I do not recommend trotting out three foreign languages, even in spots, in next Sunday's service without careful explanation and preparation over a period of time. We might be surprised though that there are those who would appreciate a larger vision of Christ's body and what it means to be the people of God! I know that persons who speak other languages are not always available although many congregations may be less tonguetied than we think.

The church in Saspamco and Muleshoe and Argyle is irrevocably linked with all points East and West, South and North. Given the God of Creation, the God of Jonah, the God of Exodus and Easter, the God in which there is neither Jew nor Greek, slave nor free, male nor female, how can we minister apart from Chile, Afghanistan, Northern Ireland, El Salvador, South Africa? A deeper pilgrimage, a closer walk, a profound journey with the One who not only has an international education, but an international presence and purpose. A gift and a challenge for the people of God!

Global Consciousness Enriches, Enlarges, and Enlivens our Concept and Our Experience of the Church and Its Mission. Belonging to a worldwide community with a redemptive purpose can provide a sense of dignity and significance to church members. The quality of life is uplifted as we remember that our story is an ancient one, a global one, and one with a future, that our lives are forever part of God's life and action. Life is enriched as we recall the variety of Christians, the countless human beings who have been baptized, and the weekly observance of the Eucharist around the world. The morale of the clergy can receive a global transfusion, not as an escape from Ida Grove or Kunkletown or Chillecothe, but as a reminder that ours *is* a worldwide gospel, a worldwide connection, a journey in the footprints and handprints of the One who imprints *all* of creation. Faith calls to faith as we hear of the sacrifices and sufferings of other Christians around the world. The depth and the quality of our lives cannot be separated from the depth and quality of our commitments and loyalties.

The Preaching Context:
A Globally Informed Liturgy

The what and the why of global consciousness have been at the center of our attention in this chapter thus far. But *what* and *why* always yearn for the *how*, that is, for tangible and visible expression. Preaching is part of the liturgy by which God and the church interact in giving and receiving. So on the way to preaching from global consciousness we need first to consider a few contours of a globally informed liturgy.

Whatever else it may be, the church is first and last a community that gathers to worship God, to remember, rehearse, re-present, and re-appropriate the Good News of God's everlasting and unconditional love in Jesus Christ. If the church is not *lost* in wonder, love, and praise, as Charles Wesley authored in "Love Divine, All Loves Excelling,"[9] the church will not be *found* in service, sacrifice, and sanctification. If the core of Christian worship is God acting to give God's life to humanity and to bring us to partake of that life, then surely the liturgy—whether written, oral, or verbal—in one way or another will be informed by global images and concerns.

Liturgy as the work of the people is more than participation in the moment of corporate worship, and more
than the planning and preparation of liturgy. Liturgy as the
work of the people is the connection between liturgy and
life, the practice of the liturgy in the world. In other words,
the liturgy is intended to be the script, the story out of which
we are called to live as members of the body of Christ in
the world. This connection between liturgy and service is
further underscored and supported by the fact that the
Greek words in the New Testament for liturgy and service—
leitourgia and *diakonia*—can constitute an interchangeable
unity in Paul's thought.

A biblically sound liturgy will avoid an imperative of
program or project, yet call for participation in the suffering of God and humanity as the work of the people. A
faithful and creative liturgy will expand moral imagination,
encourage movement toward others in their need, lift up
faith symbols and images that focus on the remembrance
of Christ's outreaching love, and point toward the Kingdom
or Rule of God that calls into question every form of bondage and servitude. We do well to remember the direction
for liturgy envisioned by Massey Shepherd, Jr., "The liturgy
exists primarily to inform a Christian's vocation in the
world and to set him (her) on fire for mission."[10]

Our present baptism rituals express the impartiality of
God's grace and thus of inclusion in the family of Christ.
Throughout our sacramental liturgies the redemptive grace
of God is a powerful force for human liberation in the sense
that it is unconditional and unmerited. As liturgical theologians, we need to interpret these implications so that
worshippers are aware of them.

There is no better example of a global perspective than
the Eucharist itself. Hopefully increasing numbers of Christians are becoming acutely aware that to share in the universal body of Christ is more than an ecclesiastical Sunday
morning exercise involving bread and juice or wine. To
participate in the broken loaf of our Lord's body is to raise
the question of a universal community—which is to raise
the question of our common humanity and thus the dilemma of the extreme disparity between the affluent and the

hungry—which is finally, at least in part, an economic and political matter. Inevitably, an insightful interpretation of God's universal grace—the bedrock of all Christian theology—will propel us into the midst of concern for a global commitment. To make the connection between liturgy and life remains a key assignment of the pastor.

Does the liturgy encourage narrow images of Camelot or does the liturgy throb and pulsate with the signs of the Covenant? Here is an example of a eucharistic invitation which lifts up a global Kingdom or Rule of God commitment.

> Come, Come!
> Come and celebrate the supper of the Lord.
> Let's make an enormous loaf of bread
> Let's bring abundant wine,
> Like the wedding at Cana.
>
> Women, don't forget the salt.
> Men, bring along the yeast.
> Come, guests. Come, many guests!
> You who are lame, blind, crippled, poor.
>
> Come quickly!
> Let's follow the recipe our Lord gave us.
> All of us, let's knead the dough together
> with our hands
> See how the bread rises,
> Watch with joy.
>
> For today we celebrate a meeting with our Lord.
> Today we renew our commitment to the Kingdom.
> Nobody should go hungry any more.[11]

By sensitive explanation of our existing liturgies, Christian liturgists can draw out their universal implications. Some of this task can be done in preaching and some in occasional step-by-step commentary as the people participate in the Sunday morning liturgy, whether it be Scripture, prayers, calls to worship, responsive lessons, or music through anthems and hymns. If what is said and done on Sunday morning is to be carried out into the week by the congregation, its meaning needs to be broken open on Sunday morning with the help of the liturgical director (pastor). In addition we can utilize liturgical forms from around the world such as the invitation for commitment by Elsa Tamez cited above.

Preaching from and for Global Consciousness

A global vision is the ultimate redefinition of our Camelot. Our tendency to define our existence by drawing a neat and tidy circle around ourselves and around the selective limits of our caring is laid bare in exposure. At the same time a global sense of story and participation in a cause greater than ourselves involving people of many lands and cultures can be incredibly freeing and enabling. Such is the purpose of preaching from a global vision.

Our globally informed sermons may be a summons to a more mature faith, a call to broader horizons and loyalties. Our preaching seeks to educate the laity with whom we serve in the world mission and outreach of the church and invite their prayerful and personal participation. A homily of global perspective can work hand in hand with congregational connections across the world. For example, the congregation in which our family is involved has formed a "Peace Partners" relationship with the Maria Madre de los Pobres congregation in San Salvador. Six members of the Northaven United Methodist Church in Dallas were commissioned in corporate worship by the congregation to travel to El Salvador in order to establish liaison between the two churches. For our purposes here it is appropriate simply to say that the worship and preaching have been important links in the North-South partnership by giving visible expression and continuity to the relationship.

To be truly global we need to cultivate opportunities to hear preaching from representatives of other countries. A lay catechist from El Salvador or a Nico Smith from South Africa (chapter 2) can shrink the world into our psyche and reveal the work of God and the faith community with great effectiveness. Camelot takes on a different dimension when we hear firsthand the faith and life struggle of Christians who live under oppression and tyranny, yet under the Lordship of Jesus Christ. There is no substitute for personalizing global connections however and wherever it takes place.

There are close connections between preaching for holistic transformation and preaching from and for global consciousness. Much that was said in the preceding chapter regarding personal motivation, biblical grounding, and theological reflection applies similarly to this chapter's concern for a global perspective. One might say that preaching from and for a global vision is preaching for holistic transformation with a global face.

Some images of preaching from a global consciousness have become my sermon titles such as these through the years: The Global Movement of the Spirit Today; Living out of a Global Awareness; God's Blessed Disturbance: Our Profoundest Hope; The Christ of the Unwanted Neighbor; A Story Larger Than Our Own; Jesus Christ: Friend of Sinners, Friend of Sufferers, Friend of Samaritans.

As in the case of preaching related to social concerns, preaching from a global perspective may emerge from a text with less than obvious global implications. For instance, take the Zacchaeus story in Luke 19:1–10, which I call "Zacchaeus' New Ambition." I think this text is especially interesting because Zacchaeus is one of the very few affluent persons in the Gospels who responds to Jesus affirmatively. That is one surprise. There is another one just around the corner. Jesus befriends a rich outcast, a despised tax collector, instead of a poor outcast.

The story focuses on the striking contrast between the surly and complaining attitude of the crowd and the joyful, accepting response of Zacchaeus. The tables are turned, so to speak, and the pious orthodox are scandalized. No one, not even a rich tax collector, is beyond the reach of transforming grace. Yet those who deny the grace of God to others cut themselves off from God's grace.

We see and hear the freedom and initiative of God's grace to restore life-in-community for the affluent Zacchaeus. We are told that grace brought forth gratitude which in turn issued forth in generosity. We are told in so many words that Zacchaeus's Camelot was audited to the quick, that there was a turning around, a new direction involving reaching out to others in a Covenant relationship. Indeed, the text as preserved by the church states, "Today salvation has come to this house since he is also a son of Abraham," (vs. 9). Abraham? Abraham implies risk, new trust, new future.

The message heard by Zacchaeus from the inviting, initiating Christ was this: "If you choose to be bound by your small Camelot and are not responsive to the suffering of the poor, I will take my life and give it to someone else." It should not be difficult to see twentieth-century North America and the present-day church therein as analogous to Zacchaeus, the tax collector whose wealth and privileged position of Camelot have been accumulated in part at the expense of others. Nor should it be difficult to draw out the Good News that God is the self-invited guest in our self-imposed Camelots, beckoning us into the Covenant by which the good life is redefined into an Abraham-Sarah journey.

If we have a deepened sensitivity for a global vision, we will be able to connect our listeners to the inherent movement from Camelot to Covenant of both lectionary and freely chosen texts.[12] Have you tried preaching about Jonah recently, that great story of international drama? Who said "love our enemies, love the undeserving, love the unrighteous" is not in the Old Testament? Or the moving and amazing intercultural saga of Ruth and Naomi? And how about a homily on Psalm 82 where Yahweh condemns the other gods to die because they are not doing their job of giving justice to the weak, rescuing the needy, and maintaining the right of the afflicted and the destitute?

Have you paid a homiletical visit lately to the Lord's Prayer? *Our* Father . . . *our* daily bread . . . *our* trespasses . . . no single Camelot pronouns here . . . the plural emphasis of the Covenant community permeates the prayer. This will preach!

Or try the Parable of the Last Judgment—Matthew 25—from a national and global standpoint as well as the personal. Robert McAfee Brown reminds us in his book *Unexpected News* that the text says, "Before him will be gathered all the *nations* . . . and he will separate them one from another."[13] Dare we bump our national priorities and policies up against this poignant identification of Christ himself with our neighbors in greatest need? Do we not have it from a reliable source that to whom much is given, much is required? Global consciousness comes dressed as both gift and challenge, as mercy and as judgment, which finally are the two sides of the same coin of God's love.

The Christian pulpit is the arena where Camelot is redefined because the global Covenant of God comes forever calling.

Part II

Naming the Reality of Preaching

Chapter Five

The Exasperation of Preaching

Preaching's social conscience cannot be separated from the task of preaching in its entirety. The particular always needs to be seen within the framework of the whole. The following two chapters reflect on the reality of preaching in both the woe and weal.

The truth about preaching is often told in letters from former students to mentors in the academy. From the front lines of homiletical struggle came this word about the preacher's dilemma and delight:

> The Conference sermon was extremely well received. I rose to fame in twenty minutes! Many said on the evaluation that it was a high point of conference. I was scared to death by not being able to start writing til 7 a.m. (service at 8:30 a.m.!). Now that is scary. But after staying up most of the night, not to mention struggling during prior days, at 7 a.m. I was able to write and it flowed out in one long stream. What do you do about that, oh teacher of preaching? Help!
>
> My church is wonderful. The people are caring and

attentive. My house is more than comfortable. The
church office is new. I love the area.

If I didn't have to *get sermons* it would be paradise.[1]

The sense of near impalement on the horns of joy
expressed by this pastor precisely states the anatomy of
preaching from head to toe: ambivalence, exhaustion, excitement, exasperation, exhilaration. Preaching is God-
wrestling activity, a joy and woe "woven fine."[2] Preachers
who casually speak of the ease of preaching are seldom
worth hearing. Those who speak only of the drudgery of
preaching are aching for a fresh epiphany of vision and
empowerment.

Yet when we name reality we gain strength for the task
because the cards are squarely on the table. The demons
usually seem less frightening and controlling when they are
stared at eye to eye, especially when we can do so with
companions who share the same hope. No dragons can be
slain or even fought to a standstill unless clearly seen and
acknowledged. By getting inside the potential downside of
preaching we can de-escalate the fantasy level and yet
glimpse the upside.

With no claim for an exhaustive inventory I nonetheless
lift up homiletical demons that I have known for more than
a quarter century. I have reason to believe the same demons
have approached my pulpit colleagues as well. But as I
allude to demons, have I not also spoken of preaching as
wrestling with God? To be sure. Zorba the Greek said, "The
Lord is a clever devil!" And Jacob at the Jabbok (Gen. 32)
wrestled with One not clearly labeled or neatly defined
beyond ambiguity. The work of the pulpit leads to an in-
timate association with this One so often concealed and
revealed simultaneously. Here is what it is like.

Wrestling with the Likes of Eliphaz, Zedekiah, and Syntyche

How would you like to spend the rest of your working
life becoming knowledgeable about an ancient document

from a different culture, with a prescientific world view and a vast array of literary genres? Not that you have to work at this every single day, just every single week except for vacations and possibly guest preacher weeks. The study of this written source is not simply for your own curiosity or information, but in order to equip you to *interpret and proclaim the message* to other human beings on a weekly basis.

There are sixty-six individual "books" within this document ranging from a couple of pages to almost a hundred and covering hundreds of years of oral and written development. Contrasting theories of origin, transmission, and interpretation abound, as do the varieties of available manuscripts in Hebrew and Greek from which the many and varied English translations have come. It is not at all unusual to find lifelong biblical scholars with diametrically opposed views on many issues.

More specifically, what are you going to do with the Lord having regard for Abel and his offering but not for Cain and his offering; or the Lord seeking to kill Moses; or the Psalmist who delights in the thought of the offspring of Zion's enemies being dashed against the rocks; or God condemning other gods to die like princes; or with a Word that was in the beginning, yet born of a virgin in Palestine; with resurrection and ascension and raising of the dead?

The worker in the vineyard of homiletics will labor for a harvest with the visible tools of various translations, commentaries, concordances, and theological dictionaries. The total preaching process will include an array of exegetical procedures such as textual, historical, literary, and form studies ("criticism"), all designed to "get inside" the ancient document which constitutes the foundation of our preaching.

When we say yes to the preaching call we sign up for an ongoing lifetime connection with an ancient document. It is a demanding discipline for which there is no long-range substitute of human cleverness or theological sophistication. The preaching ministry is a "book" profession calling for continuing reading and reflection. The Bible is our "book of books," our constant touchstone for all the far corners of ordained ministry. If you tire easily of research and "sleuthing" bygone places and characters for contemporary recalling and interpretation, the preaching ministry is not for you.

When I was a seminary student in the mid-fifties, the preaching textbooks were usually of Scottish descent: James Stewart's *Heralds of God*, James Cleland's *The True and Lively Word*, and *The Making of the Sermon* by Robert McCracken. Hermeneutics and homiletics have travelled some distance since those days, but not beyond Stewart's memorable ode to the necessity of being yoked to Scripture as a preacher:

> If you preach your own theories and ideas, using Scripture texts merely as a peg to hang them on, you will soon be at the end of your resources—and the sooner the better. But if you will let the Scriptures speak their own message, if you will realize that every passage or text has its own quite distinctive meaning, you will begin to feel that the problem is not lack of fresh material, but the very embarrassment of riches.[3]

Biblical study is not optional for those who would speak for God. Wrestling with places such as the banks of the river Jabbok, Nebo, the country of the Gerasenes, Capernaum, Cana, Corinth, and Ephesus, to say nothing of Bethlehem and Nazareth, encompasses the territory of the faithful exegete. And getting acquainted with such characters as Eliphaz, Zedekiah, and Syntyche is part of the traveling orders of the pulpit on the move.

Taking the Pulse of the Saints in Saspamco and the Surrounding Territory

A quality of absurdity accompanies our attempts to grade sermons in the academic classroom. The reason is clear enough. How can we possibly assess a sermon apart from the life context of a congregation? How can we evaluate what might be taking place in communication in a setting which is divorced from the relationship between preacher/pastor/person and people?[4] How can we separate preaching from real, live worship? We in the academy need to acknowledge the artificial setting of classrooms and do the best we can. At least every student is under a similar disadvantage!

Would-be preachers are called to exegete the congregation's story as well as the covenantal story transmitted in Scripture. Thus the first activity of preaching is not speaking but listening. Listen to the history and the immediacy of this congregation. Listen to the pulse of the times in the wider community.

I like to show a film to my students called *I Heard the Owl Call My Name*, based on Margaret Craven's novel.[5] A young Episcopal seminary graduate is sent to a Native American congregation located on one of the islands off the Pacific Northwest mainland. The bishop, who served the parish early in his own ministry, says to the fledgling minister-to-be, "Mark, you are well read. You are bright. You are a good student. Mark, you know nothing."

As events unfold in his new parish, Mark learns by trial and error how to minister in a setting alien to his own upbringing. The people literally teach him how to understand their history, their story, their hopes and fears. His initial preaching is alienating because he has not yet listened and learned how to connect the Covenant story with the congregational story. As did Jacob at Bethel he discovered over a period of time that surely God was in this place.

In *Roots* Alex Haley wrote of the African griots, the aged storytellers who knew the history of the people.[6] When we preachers dash into town, we had better seek out the various stories of these particular people. Spend some time with Austa Wyrick, the eighty-seven-year-old across the street from the parsonage. Seek out Charlie Sims on the courthouse square. You will be learning about the town, the parish, the people. Have a hamburger at Presto's Dairy Queen so you can absorb some wisdom from Presto, the blind proprietor. He will teach you how to grapple with limitations, how to see life from a different perspective. Or, in suburban ministry, schedule some lunchtime visits with working people where possible. They will update you on local events.

Put itineracy to work within the parish and you will

begin to experience the past and the present of the local saints: the contours of class and racial alienation; the daily heroism of people contending with life in spite of a seemingly stacked deck; the poignancy of depopulated towns groaning with farm crises and a sense of better days gone by, yet amenable to the sounds of dignity and hope; the primary language of individualism[7] which grips our common ethos, yet the longing for a sense of community which draws out our most decent instincts.

Faithful biblical study is the home plate of the preaching endeavor. But sermons do not become sermons until the past of the biblical story connects with present-day parishioners. And that will happen as we become listeners, social critics, and pulse takers of life in local, national, and global neighborhoods. Observe, analyze, discern, diagnose, prescribe; it is all part of the homiletical territory.

A seminary student once remarked to me that a theological education is like having all your nerve endings exposed. "You are never the same again because the injustices and hurt of the world become clearer. We are drawn into a heightened awareness and sensitivity calling us to lean into the world's pain. And there is no reversal of this raised consciousness."

You want to be a preacher? We are told that we must have something to say, yes. But in order to open our mouths intelligently and faithfully we must have something to hear. That something is the pulsebeat of life in the surrounding world. Look next door. Listen to "marginalized" people near and far. The first rule of preaching is *turn up your hearing aid*.

Living With Uncertain, Intangible Results

What difference does preaching make? The homiletical bottom line is not as measurable as some types of work. Profits, sales, and expenses are quantifiable. *Meaning* in people's lives is usually more difficult to assess. A sacramental perception of human existence that depends on divine grace is not easily calibrated. Neither are the mysteries of God for which preachers are interpreters.

A steady post-sermon chorus of "enjoyed your sermon" may be alternately interpreted as a euphemistic ho-hum, a kind-hearted "nice try," or as a sign that the Word has once again become flesh through the combination of God's grace and faithful sermonic discipline. Which? We seldom know unless more specifics are forthcoming.

In spite of the sense of well-being when all the pews or chairs are filled, we know—unless we hide it from ourselves—that these visible signs are not guarantees of the authenticity of our preaching. One can point to many situations today where crowds respond to mercantile preaching and where more substantial preaching is less populated. The ambiguity of uncertain results is part and parcel of preaching. It is probably a blessing in disguise as it prevents us from becoming dependent on ego-trips as our reward. Martin Luther had an extremely valuable word for every generation of preachers: "To preach the Gospel for praise is bad business, especially when people stop praising you. Find your praise in the testimony of a good conscience."[8]

Maybe the reason that not a few clergypersons are experts at carpentry and related skills has to do with more than economic thrift or messianic complexes: they like doing something relatively manageable and concrete, at least occasionally.

It Seems As If Every Worshipper Hears a Different Sermon

An ancient adage in homiletics claims that the preacher preaches three sermons on each occasion: the sermon intended, the sermon actually preached, and the sermon (in retrospect) wishfully preached. A similar adage applies on the hearing level. As worshippers we bring our own hearing devices determined by our current life situation. We hear our own version of what is said and interpret it accordingly. While this is frequently an indispensable aid to the preaching event, we preachers are sometimes not wise enough to see it as such.

We become exasperated when people not only seem to hear a message different from that which others hear but also hear something quite at odds with what we intended to be heard. If we reflect for a moment on Lawrence Kohlberg's stages of moral development, on Carol Gilligan's different voices, and on James Fowler's stages of faith, we come to realize the incredible variety of ears that compose the hearing sensorium.[9] Add further the so-called left-brainer on the third row who is geared to the sixteenth-century print revolution, preferring the high definition communication of well-defined, three-point sermons characterized by predictable, sequential, cumulative process. Add still further the right-brainer in the balcony who is geared to the twentieth-century electronic revolution, preferring low definition communications of the intuitive, the imaginative, the inductive, the element of surprise, and less closure. By such consideration of our hearers we come to the renewed awareness that there is more we do not control than we do, and that worshippers will hear and participate on their own terms. This is an exasperating circumstance for our clerical drive to be in control. Ironically, it is the circumstance that makes preaching possible.

Dispensing a Disposable Art Form:
Cost versus Benefit

Artists of the visual have something to show for their efforts. The sweat and tears of discipline, the edge of the creative abyss, the joy of visual development issue forth in sculpture, painting, banners, and other objects remaining in overt form. Their efforts may or may not be appreciated but at least the results are "there."

Preaching is in the genre of performing arts (this news will be a shock to some, perhaps many!). Yet when the final amen is pronounced, whether literally or figuratively, nothing remains in discernible form, unless, of course, the ser-

80536

mon is taped or printed for distribution. Since over a period of time preparation for preaching will consume more time than any other single endeavor of ministry, the homiletician is bound to ask, "Is the benefit worth the cost?" The cost is measured in terms of time necessary for responsible preparation and in terms of the time not thereby available for other ministries or for family and leisure time. There will be weeks when time spent on pastoral care other than preaching will exceed that given to homiletical process. There will be times when administrative duties will be most prominent. But over the long haul I expect preaching preparation will demand the most time as it progresses throughout the week toward a definitive time and place.

There are no easy answers for this frequent "Catch-22" issue for ordained clergy in the preaching ministry. The costs are considerable but in the long run the benefits will seem greater for those who theologically cannot do otherwise. You will have realized several subheads ago that the exasperations and burdens of preaching cannot be separated from the exhilarations and blessings.

Ready or Not! A Relentless Discipline of Schedule

The weekly preaching assignment is a relentless discipline. A nationally known football coach once said that in his business "humility is always just seven days away." So it is with preaching. Every seven days, whether you feel like it or not, regardless of two funerals, a wedding, a breakdown of your car, family budget problems, and an uncooperative runny nose, the moment is approaching. So at the appointed time on Sunday, you prepare not just to give a talk, but audaciously and humbly to speak for God as the voice of God. If this sounds like too high a definition of preaching, remember that we are *not* called to speak for ourselves or strictly from our own resources.

During my fifteen years in the local pastorate I had two fantasies regarding release from the weekly discipline. One is that we could have inherited the Aztec calendar adapted from the Mayans of 600 B. C. who had calculated 365.242

LINCOLN CHRISTIAN COLLEGE AND SEMINARY

days in a year. The Aztecs adopted this solar year and divided it into eighteen weeks of twenty days, with five extra days at the end of each year. Think of it! Eighteen sermons per year over twenty-day intervals. But knowing my human condition—and probably yours—the temptation to procrastinate would simply be spread over more days throughout the year.

My other preaching fantasy regarding the weekly sermon had to do with preaching being accorded the status of developing poetry.

Whoever heard of a poet who had to produce on a ready-or-not treadmill? Let the preacher have adequate gestation time until the moment of rapture demands a proclamation to the people! No matter that this might take weeks or even months. My fantasy would call for ringing a giant bell (where this would be or how people would hear it is not clear) and a dramatic announcement that a divinely inspired word is about to come forth from the preacher's poetic and eloquent tongue.[10]

In *Joys and Sorrows* the great cellist Pablo Casals tells of an event which brought his first American tour to a sudden end. While climbing with friends on Mount Tamalpais in the San Francisco area, a loose boulder hurtled down the mountainside, smashing his fingering hand. "My friends were aghast. But when I looked at my mangled bloody fingers, I had a strangely different reaction. My first thought was, 'Thank God, I'll never have to play the cello again!'"

I have yet to find a preacher who does not readily understand what Casals was saying. Casals goes on to say, "The fact is that dedication to one's art does involve a sort of enslavement, and then too, of course, I have always felt such dreadful anxiety before performances."[11]

Responding to a High Level of Self-Disclosure

Preaching and presiding in worship represents the greatest visibility with the largest number of people on the most frequent and regular basis of any function of ordained ministry. Whether we appear in a robe, an alb, a suit, or a dress, we stand theologically and psychologically naked before God and congregation. Some preachers are actors in disguise and enjoy the self-disclosure. Whether we like it or not, however, preaching inevitably reveals our thought, our personality, and at least our public way of relating to others in a liturgical setting.

Whatever vocabulary may be used, preaching finally gets down to some concept of the human condition and to a view of God's action in relation to the perceived condition. Thus the preacher has no choice but to reveal in both content and style of delivery his or her way of sizing up the world and God's manner of relating to it. Is sin a condition of being or an individual act? Are some "sins" worse than others? Is the church for all people regardless of life-style and societal standing? Is God responsible for suffering, and if not, who or what is? How is the gospel related to politics? What does the Bible teach about abundant life? About death and life beyond death? About freedom and determination? In due time in her or his own way the preacher's viewpoints on these questions as interpretations of Scripture will be revealed in the homiletical process. And so will the presuppositions of the preacher about the relation of clergy and laity, and the clergy's own sense of self.

Of course self-disclosure in the pulpit is never disconnected with the revealing of self during the other six days of pastoral ministry. The pulpit disclosure is but the public focus of an ongoing representative ministry in the name of God and on behalf of the faith community.

The Erosion of Sacred Story

Most of the exasperations mentioned above are endemic to preaching itself. But there are some circumstances particularly present in this generation. These contemporary challenges to preaching have been well documented by a number of authors, especially Fred Craddock.[12] Those familiar with his writing will recall his pertinent analysis of the loss of automatic or attributive authority and the breakdown of moral consensus; the loss of word power and meaning in an age of doublespeak with the consequence that meaning is to be experienced more through deeds than talk; the change in perceiving reality from the oral to a visual entertainment culture; and the charge that preaching is outmoded communication because it is undemocratic and opposed to collegiality and process.

Closely related to the loss of authority, or perhaps a manifestation of it, is the erosion of sacred story in the memories of those to whom and for whom preaching exists. Preachers can no longer assume, if we ever could, that there is a widespread community memory bank of the corporate story in the listening congregation. This is an opportunity for preaching if we are aware of it, and certainly for the educational function of the church, but it means that preaching needs to unfold the sacred or Covenant story from the very beginning. The task is often facilitated by the memory bank of the musical heritage of the church retained long after the biblical story otherwise has been neglected and forgotten. Thus the liturgical framework for preaching affords a vehicle for memory development and restoration.

The need to restore a common memory for the worshipping congregation is a key challenge for preaching in this generation.

The Awesomeness of Speaking for God

If we encounter a person on the street or anywhere else who claims to speak for God or as the living voice of God, we immediately look for a wagon and attendants in white coats. God-language is suspect when it infers a pipeline approach to the divine or a special personal relationship.

Yet for the most part the precise claim of the church is that the aim of preaching is to be the conduit of the living voice of God. Preaching is not intended to be simply words about God but rather the Word of God, the offering of the life of God as known through Jesus Christ. Preaching has been widely understood as the lifting up of voices in the

historic apostolic succession of proclamation and participation, a means of grace by which the life, death, and resurrection of Jesus Christ are called forth as contemporary
promise and claim.

The true and lively Word faithfully preached in spite
of human frailty and limitations is often understood theologically as the re-presentation of God in Jesus Christ, as
surely as the Word preached by Paul and Peter in the
earliest church. Just as the real presence of Jesus Christ in
the Eucharist has been variously interpreted, so the con-
tinuation of Christ's presence and ministry in preaching
has been lifted up as revelatory event. *This* is the awful and
audacious legacy of preaching.

The dilemmas for the preacher are obvious. Who is
qualified to speak for God? How can we distinguish between
God's Word and our own biases and hidden agendas? Is it
not always *my* interpretation, right or wrong? Is not the
task of speaking in the name of God impossible, a seductive
trap that leads either to insufferable arrogance or to despair
in the face of a task too immense and overwhelming? With
these questions on our lips it is time to consider the exhilaration of preaching.

Chapter Six

The Exhilaration of Preaching

Through the years I have become convinced that the mix of woe and weal in preaching is just about the most outlandish blend of beatitude and bedevilment yet invented by the mysterious Divine Mind. No wonder there is an ancient bit of wisdom handed down through the centuries from ecclesiastical sages. Simply put, their counsel is this: "If you can do anything else, for God's sake, and for the sake of yourself and others, do it!"

So the company of preachers constitutes a community of those who cannot do anything else! Of course there are critics who say we enter the ordained ministry because we cannot do anything else. I trust they are mistaken in a practical sense, but theologically speaking they are absolutely correct, even if they do not know it.

C. S. Lewis's Screwtape[1] would say the desire for good preaching and the difficulty of good preaching are sufficiently frustrating to drive both congregation and preacher into the conniving hands of the devil. Yet there is that tantalizing possibility of listener and preacher alike being touched again by the promise and claim of God's unconditional love through the act of preaching. And somehow in ways beyond our knowing, to live the unlivable and to love the unlovable and to change the unchangeable once again becomes an open agenda. Preaching always bears potential significance, because at its best it has to do with the very heart and soul of life.

Let me suggest what the relationship between the exasperation and the exhilaration of preaching can be like.

The Rocky Mountain High
of Apostolic Compulsion

> Even before a word is on my tongue, lo, O Lord, Thou knowest it altogether.
>
> Thou dost beset me behind and before, and layest Thy hand upon me. . . .
>
> Thy eyes beheld my unformed substance; in thy book were written, every one of them, the days that were formed for me, when as yet there was none of them (Ps. 139:4, 5, 16).

Talk with those who are convinced of a call to the preaching ministry and you will hear echoes of predestiny. It was meant to be; in retrospect it could not have been otherwise, regardless of how long we may have resisted the call. Preaching is the fulfillment of a purpose, a plan, a process initiated by the Not-me, the Not-you, and the Not-all-of-us-put-together. Crazy? Absurd? Maybe so. But try to convince any preacher otherwise who has been called. The sense of meant-to-be-ness is not to be denied.

Gary Johnson, a former seminary student who is also a poet and musician in his own right, spoke for generations of the called with these words on the wings of destiny:

> Isaiah was called by the Lord in a vision
> An awesome and glorious scene
> And he heard the Lord ask, whom shall I send?
> And he said, "Here am I, send me"
> And down through the ages the words of
>   those pages
> Have burned so many like me
> Who in fear and trembling, Isaiah resembling
> Say Lord, Here am I, send me
>
> > I wish I could say it happened the way
> > It did when Isaiah was called
> > Miraculous visions or heavenly voices
> > Like Moses or Mary or Paul

But that's not how it is, no nothing like that
Has ever happened to me
No doves descending, no angels defending
No trances, no tongues, no dreams

It's just something inside, that can't be denied
Something that's always been there
It's hard to explain, I can't give it a name
It came from I know not where
It used to scare me and make me feel crazy
I could not control it at all
Something so deep and so strong and so free
Something that answers the call.

When I first said
"I'm called," my friends were appalled
And my family just sat there and stared
My wife started to cry and I don't think that I
Have ever been quite so scared
Part of me wanted to run and hide
And pretend that it just wasn't so
And part of me felt like the prodigal son
Who quit running and finally came home

When I open the pages and read of Isaiah
I get goosebumps all over my skin
And I know that it's true, he had it too
That same something within, then God's
Greatness astounds me, God's power surrounds me
God's presence electrifies me
Then in fear and trembling, Isaiah resembling
I say "Here am I, send me."[2]

To be sure our love affair with the weekly practice of preaching waxes and wanes like the coming and going of the tides—dryness, excitement; lack of inspiration, the nightingale sings again; not Sunday already, can't wait to preach—and so it goes. But underneath it all is the silently running subterranean stream of an invitation and an inevitability to preach.

Our early church ancestors spoke of the apostolic compulsion, the *necessity* of preaching come what may. We *must* speak of what we have seen and heard. But long before the new Covenant, those pushed and pulled by the God of the former Covenant spoke of the homiletical inevitability:

> If I say "I will not mention him, or speak any more in his
> name," there is in my heart as it were a burning fire shut
> up in my bones, and I am weary with holding it in, and I
> cannot (Jeremiah 20:9).

You can call it passion, you can call it obsession, you can call
it the inevitability of destiny, or the apostolic compulsion.
Whichever it is, it is the fulfillment of our being, both
theologically and psychologically. Faithfulness is also its
name.

The Covenant and Company of Foolish Preachers

As preachers we do not stand alone, theologically, his-
torically, or psychologically. We stand on the promises, the
premises, and the presence of a preaching community with
roots as far back as the Hebrew prophets and as contemporary as our present-day colleagues in the preaching ministry.

To our own detriment we preachers have tended to
isolate ourselves in a hermetically sealed homiletical bub-
ble. Preaching has been reduced to weekly solo flights lack-
ing the support of the faith community both past and present. The sermon is treated as an intelligence agency type
secret, carefully hoarded until delivery time. No wonder
the sermon process becomes burdensome.

All of us in the preaching ministry are members of the
Order of Preachers (O.P.), as the Dominicans refer to themselves. We stand in the apostolic succession of voices lifted
up in a historical chorus of heralds and harbingers of Good
News. We do not reinvent the preaching wheel on a weekly
basis; we carry on in an uninterrupted line of preachers
who in the name of the gospel call forth life amid the
conditions of death, wholeness amid sickness, truth amid
falsehood, and voice amid the conditions of silence.

My teaching colleague, Zan W. Holmes, Jr., is fond of
saying that he "stacks his gallery" with favorite theologians
and preachers when he preaches, as well as special lay
persons. They are "present" both in the preparation and
the preaching of the sermon. This special "communion of

saints" surrounds and uplifts preaching so that it is part of a larger whole. Just as traditional homiletical wisdom encourages the locating of some friendly faces in the congregation during sermon delivery, so we are to remember and recall those special saints whose presence undergirds and sustains our preaching efforts.

One of the great advances in present-day exegetical and homiletical practice is the growing number of clergy groups who meet regularly to discuss the lectionary texts for the coming week(s). If I had my local church ministry before me again, I would seek out the give and take of lectionary conversations with other clergy in order to multiply the educational and experiential resources for preaching. Nowhere is our North American individualism expressed more clearly than in our lack of a collegial, communal approach to biblical interpretation. We preach community but we seldom seem to practice what we preach when it comes to the vehicle which advocates community formation!

The tradition to which we belong is of God; it has a long line of splendor before our advent and will remain when our last sermon has run out of congregational memory. Archbishop Oscar Romero of El Salvador, assassinated in March 1980 while celebrating the mass, put our preaching into perspective: "The Word remains. This is the great comfort of one who preaches. My voice will disappear, but my word, which is Christ, will remain. . . ."[3] Heaven and earth will pass away, and only the Word remains. The Word we preach is a Word for all seasons and for all time. Faith comes from what is heard, and what is heard comes by the preaching of Christ (Rom. 10:17). And the preaching of Christ is the sine qua non of the company of preachers.

The Church Confessing Its Faith:
Easter Re-Presented

Few Christians would argue with the notion that the church is called into being by the gospel, or at the very least, that the church is the historical, empirical result. My first New Testament teacher, John Knox, then of Union Theological Seminary in New York, was fond of saying that the only thing we have after Jesus Christ that we did not have before his coming is the church. Those who affirmed Jesus as Christ were formed by the living Word into a Covenant community even as their literary response formed the written Word constituting an ongoing recorded witness to Jesus Christ.

What is sometimes less evident, or at least less remembered, is that the church also forms the gospel. The gospel is not a timeless truth or world view existing in a vacuum or even as a static written document. As Martin Luther put it, faith is an acoustical affair which happens again and again in response to hearing the Word. For the sixteenth-century reformers, at least, the Word of God was above all a preached Word. The Word could not be separated from its proclamation.

The late Ronald E. Sleeth gave particular attention in some of his published works to the identification of preaching with the gospel itself. Quoting a range of theologians (H. H. Farmer, Emil Brunner, Rudolf Bultmann, and P. T. Forsyth, for example), Sleeth reminded his readers that preaching is the function by which the promise and the claim of Jesus Christ is continued, that one cannot separate the means of witnessing to the message (preaching) from the content of the message itself.[4]

In fairness, we need to realize that not every Christian tradition shares the primacy of preaching articulated by the sixteenth-century Reformers and their followers by whatever name. The core of Quaker tradition would provide us with a quite different view of the place of preaching. Also, the Disciples of Christ, while not disregarding the significance of preaching, would suggest that the Lord's meal is central to the worship experience. Until the Second Vatican Council (1962–1965) the homily in Roman Catholic worship was less prominent than now called for in the Constitution on the Sacred Liturgy.

Yet there remains a basic thread of agreement concerning the indispensability of preaching as a "central function for which the church exists and by which it defines itself":

The Augsburg Confession (1530) defined the "one holy Christian Church" as "the assembly of all believers among whom the Gospel is *preached* in its purity and the holy sacraments are administered according to the Gospel." The Anglican Articles of Religion (1563)—from which John Wesley excerpted the Methodist Articles (1784)—declared: "The Visible Church of Christ is a congregation of faithful men, in which the pure word of God is preached, and the Sacraments duly administered . . ." The Edinburgh Conference on Faith and Order (1937) pronounced ecumenical consensus that "It is the function of the Church to glorify God in its life and worship, to proclaim [i. e., to *preach*] the gospel to every creature. . . ." And the New Delhi Assembly of the World Council of churches (1961) saw Christ's presence in the preached word as foundational to the church's unity. "In the faithful *preaching* of the Word," the Council said, "the living Christ is present as our contemporary in every age. . . . In the human words of the preacher every new generation is confronted by the Christ as one who speaks to them where they actually are." In its preaching a denomination articulates its identity, both for its own people and for others in ecumenical consultation.[5]

While these statements by themselves provide only a partial definition of the church, they do hold before us the historic and ongoing significance in which preaching is held.

In *Preaching for Today*, Clyde E. Fant quotes Nels Ferré: "Preaching cannot take the place of the acted Word in sacrament nor the lived Word in Christian fellowship, but preaching is indispensable as the communication of the Word—the meaning and purpose of God."[6] As Fant himself says in *Preaching for Today*:

Preaching continues to have an irreplaceable position in Christian theology and Christian worship because it does what God did in His self-disclosure to Israel, in His revelation to prophets and apostles, in the fullness of His revelation in Jesus. It provides a medium for revelation which enables the eternal Word to maintain its living, dynamic character and encounter our concrete situation.[7]

These testimonies to preaching remind us that preaching is used by God to enable the church to confess its own faith and thereby to re-present the risen Christ to the faith community and to the wider community. Preaching will continue to be described in a variety of ways: proclaiming the lordship of Jesus Christ; bringing "the people before the presence of God and within sight of the heart of Christ";[8] "a manifestation of the Incarnate Word from the Written Word by the Spoken Word";[9] telling the story of God's mighty acts of salvation; the re-presentation of the ultimate promise and claim of God's everlasting and unconditional love in Jesus Christ; "the living voice of God addressing contemporary people with the good news of God's gracious judgment and judging grace in Jesus Christ."[10]

Whatever description we may use for preaching the gospel, the exhilaration for the preacher resides in the experience of serving as the representative agent through whom the church more fully becomes the church. No one else in church or society is trained for this function of proclamation by which the church, as many of us understand it, comes into being.

In spite of the utterly subjective nature of preaching, there is an objective transference of meaning inherent in the act of preaching. My wife, Fran, helped me to see inside this truth through her comparison of hearing me in the pulpit and hearing me "in person" informally. "It's not the same," she says. "In the act of preaching you're you, but it's more than you. It's like a word from elsewhere, a given for which you are the medium."

As the gospel forms the church, so the preaching of the church forms the gospel as contemporary event, calling for decision and response.

In Spite of All: The Power of Word and Words

We preach at the intersection of word devaluation and word reevaluation. The devaluation may be traced to multiple sources.[11] Television has made us skeptical of "messages" telling us of everything from the one true deodorant to the right choice in communication systems. Only a zealot-like intentionality to see a program to its conclusion can withstand the onslaught of inane commercial babblings.

The exchange rate on the spoken word is rendered cheap, so that not a few are convinced that integrity in communication comes through the efficacy of deeds and actions. The dishonesty and chicanery of certain television-based religious leaders has made a further mockery of words supposedly used as religious content.

Adding to the further deterioration of trust in words is the unfortunate doublespeak and misinformation that increasingly characterizes much of our public discourse. This state of affairs is hardly new, yet from Vietnam to Watergate to "Contragate" the occasional seems to be expanding into the frequent, a communication gap of major proportions. Former national guardsmen of the brutal Somoza regime in Nicaragua become freedom fighters; lying to the American people becomes necessary for national security; El Salvador is said to be a "democracy," in spite of clear factual evidence of military dominance and death squads in constant activity. As a prophet of long ago exclaimed, "Truth has fallen in the public squares" (Isa. 59:14).

Simultaneous with word devaluation, however, is the recent work of communication and linguistic theorists telling us the shape of reality is verbal.[12] Years ago Paul Tillich reminded us that we can speak to others only because we have been spoken to or addressed in words. Verbal symbols constitute the basis of human community and of humanity itself. The centrality of the spoken word does not deny the power of touch and other senses, nor the power of observation. Rather the spoken word is so basic to our everyday existence that we simply take its importance for granted, even when we lament the lack of integrity or trustworthiness of words.

Imagine for a moment life without spoken words on a global basis over the past two thousand years as it might relate to the development of Judeo-Christian faith—speechless prophets and priests, a wordless Jesus, acts of the apostles with no preaching, no verbal witnessing. Now carry this through to our time. Even this very limited exercise boggles the mind. It may be hard at times to live with words as they misdirect, wound, and confuse. But it is certainly unthinkable to live on an extended basis without the fundamental building blocks of human communication.

Since preaching is a focused event in time and place which seeks to connect in words *the* story with our story, it has a way of fueling and giving direction to the total witness of the congregation. The story told from the pulpit in both its content and style tends either to energize or enervate the life of the faith community.

Preaching weaves a fabric of meaning over a period of time, preserving with the liturgy the sacred story, recalling the sacred memory, and making connections with the story of the congregation and of the members who make up the congregation. Words are symbols that are like seeds in the soil of the soul, developing a life of their own over a period of time.

I never cease to be amazed how bits and pieces of sermons reside for years—even a lifetime—in the human consciousness. Perhaps it is only a sermon title and main idea, or maybe a single phrase, that arrested attention and lodged itself securely in a person's memory as a faith companion through thick and thin. "Do you remember the sermon you preached seven years ago when you said . . . ?" asks the former parishioner at a chance meeting. The truth is you do not but you give thanks for the memory—not yours, but the parishioner's. And you give further thanks for the power of the Word—not yours, but God's, through your words.

There is yet a more intriguing, yet fairly common, phenomenon that bears witness to the power of Word and words. Someone tells you with unmitigated enthusiasm, "I have just heard a marvelous and moving sermon." Naturally your curiosity is pricked, so you ask, "What was said that was so exciting?" You really want to know out of joy for your friend, but you also wonder if there might be a word for you as person *and* as preacher of next week's sermon.

It took me about fifteen years, being a slow learner in this respect, to realize that the chance of a coherent cognitive answer is about thirty percent. More likely comes the reply with a puzzled look, "Well, I really can't tell you exactly." Pause. Then may come a very brief general account, concluded by the reassurance, "It was memorable and powerful. It made a difference." End of conversation.

What does this mean? It means that we are caught up in the fabric of meaning, the field of consciousness, through the power of words become Word, yet without being able to remember many exact words. Some years after the death of my parents I was startled and initially bothered when I first realized how few of their words I could remember verbatim. After all we had been around each other off and on for quite a few years. Of course, "Let's rip, ravel, and tear" came to mind, my Dad's usual saying when I was a child as we were going on vacation in the car. And Mom's plaintive "Don't grieve for me" (as though this were possible!) when she was in the advanced stage of dying with cancer. And a few other recurring or random sayings.

Though particular words from a sermon will on occasion remain in the memories of individuals, after some reflection I came to realize that the words mattered much less than "the Incarnate Word" of their total lives. That is, I could tell you who they were, what they meant to me, and where they stood on just about any matter. Their many words were absorbed into the larger fabric of meaning which itself constituted a word of life. This is what preaching is finally about. Not that individual words are unimportant. They are very important, our conveyors of the sermon. But no matter how much we love words—and preachers need to!—and regardless of how well crafted our words may be, they point to a larger Word that becomes flesh in the preaching event. Our listeners remember the Word. Or is it closer to truth to say that the Word remembers us? Exhilaration is concomitant of the Word and its words!

Embracing Sparrows and Systems

Not everyone will agree that the challenge to preach to both individuals and to powers and principalities belongs in the inventory of homiletical hilarity and excitement. As we have explored in chapters 3 and 4, we cannot separate

concern for individuals and the gospel-based role of creative social critic. When we take on issues we also take on
the impact of the social matrix of individuals. When we
reach out to individuals we are inevitably connecting with
the larger communal scene. David Buttrick has suggested
that we never truly address individuals as individuals in
preaching even though this has been a basic presupposition
of the American pulpit for the past thirty years.[13] Thus our
preaching is always actually a message to the self in social
relationship and to the world made up of individuals.

Just as spirituality and liberation are finally of one
piece, so it is with the so-called personal and social gospel.
They are simply two ways of addressing the same reality.
Our preaching, if faithful to the Incarnate One and to the
Vulnerable-Victorious One, will offer light and hope to the
plight and flight of the sparrow and to the systemic causes
of suffering and injustice. As always the light and hope of
the gospel constitute God's loving judgment and judging
love.

Why, however, include preaching a social gospel as an
invitation to exhilaration? Because to speak the truth (as
we understand it) in love from the pulpit is a rare privilege
and opportunity of life and ministry. It goes with being
faithful and being faithful is its own reward even when it
brings rebuff or acrimony as well as appreciation and affirmation.

Archetypes for All Types

During the initial years of my ministry I nearly always
perceived the term "tradition" as having a negative con-
notation. Images of Pharisees, scribes, and elders immediately flooded my mental screen. Besides, I was much too
involved with "creative" innovations of ministry to get
trapped in antiques of the past. Gradually I learned that
while many things were new to my personal experience,
the treasury of the church's tradition already included in
different historical settings many of the experiments that
seemed so new—liturgical dance, the use of varied musical

instruments, and pioneering ventures in architecture. I also learned that the most theologically and pastorally significant innovations in any age are likely to come from those who know their church history and the traditions therein.

Through the years I have come to appreciate a very different understanding of the meaning of tradition. A particularly helpful focus came from Sallie McFague. She points out that "a person must get inside a religious tradition, be able to move around in it both comfortably and critically, love it and question it at the same time. . . . This is what formation is about—the settling of a religious tradition into the very flesh and bones of one's existence."[14]

In the paragraph above, tradition is used in a very broad sense to be inclusive of the whole range of Christian teachings in Scripture as well as the tradition of church history through the years. The formation of faith is an inevitable moving around both critically and comfortably in a tradition. By this process tradition is no longer experienced simply as a fence that walls out fresh vitality and redirection. Precisely the opposite! Tradition becomes the raw material out of which God gives to our lives story and a new future. Tradition is not a fence, but a gate to the future with hinges from the past. In fact, a true sense of tradition provides *roots* from which a future may be critically shaped, a future in which the tradition is partially accepted and partially rejected.

The historical and transcultural power of the Christian gospel is of course rooted in the tradition of God's revelation through Jesus Christ. But what is it about this story that has enabled it to penetrate the depths of the human condition? Why does this particular script, one among many, continue to unfold on a global basis? Many answers can be given. I believe that one of them—often overlooked—is because the Christian story is deeply embedded in the most profound and ultimate human experience: crucifixion and resurrection, death and life. Such archetypal images touch us with the root meaning of our experience.

The biblical narratives are frequently woven around archetypal images. A key Old Testament example is the Exodus event. It is an archetype of virtually all human struggle for growth, identity, freedom, and responsibility, whether individual or corporate. We yearn for a new future, yet its uncharted risk in the wilderness drives us to consider the safety and routine of Pharaoh's fleshpots. The dialectic of all freedom and responsibility is a variation of this narrative.

If we theologize deductively, we begin with the premise that Jesus Christ is Lord and deduce meanings from that presupposition. But if we proceed inductively by looking at human experience, we will see that it is because the Jesus Christ story is the very metabolism of our experience that it has lasting power and meaning. The good in life is forever being defeated and reborn. We are forever saying no to life and then being grasped by a yes. Life is constantly coming out of death and new beginnings emerge from our endings. And this crucifixion-resurrection comes to us as an invitation to die in order to be reborn. This is the pulsebeat of human experience. Because the anatomy of the gospel tradition and story is the anatomy of life itself, the gospel reflects the way life is for us all.

Preaching is the oralizing of biblical archetypes in all types of human conditions and cultures. When we choose our having been chosen for this audacious task, we have cast our lot with regular involvement in both the depths and the heights of divine and human experience.[15]

A Roller Coaster Journey of Self-Discovery

Preaching is a theological and psychological X ray of the preacher's soul. In the God-wrestling of the preaching process "the Word interprets us,"[16] and "the Word forms the preacher."[17] The preacher also forms the Word for better or worse from an a priori hermeneutic, that is, from the set of presuppositions and agenda which we inevitably bring to the preaching task.

In the interaction of God's Word with the preacher's world, we are offered growth in self-reflection, insight, and discernment. Over a period of time we all listen to many forebears of the faith and to some extent walk in their shoes as their journey intersects and informs and transforms our own. Preaching is self-actualization in the Word.

The preaching process has been my constant theological guide as I have wrestled with Jonah's reluctance, Jeremiah's inner struggle, the simplicity and profundity of Mary's faith, the mystery of how it is that the Suffering One became the Sovereign One. For who among us can preach a Word not already addressed to the preacher? If the Word does not grow on the preacher, how can God use us as instruments of growth for others? As preachers we are in constant theological dialogue with a host of mentors who seek to instruct our own faith and the faith we proclaim to others.

Self-discovery through preaching comes in the act of preaching as well as the exegetical and theological give and take which precedes the preaching event. We discover our style of communication and our related strengths and weaknesses. Our points of passion for the gospel are revealed to us in surprising ways. We come face to face with our need to be accepted as better than average preachers and with the puzzle of forming criteria for homiletical fidelity.

The preacher may be the academic dean, especially for the small congregation. But the truth is we never leave the classroom ourselves—the classroom of biblical study and sermon preparation, and the classroom of the sanctuary in which the preacher and people are under the tutelage of God's Word together as co-learners.

The philosopher José Ortega y Gasset once said that language is the acoustical profile of the soul of a people. Connection: liturgy is the theological, spiritual profile of the soul of a people. *Preaching* is the theological, spiritual profile of the soul of the preacher.

Gratification in the Preaching Process

Is it homiletical heresy to suggest that the whole theological range of hermeneutics and homiletics in and of itself offers at least periodic and recurring excitement, gratification, and yes, even fun? Let us hope not. If it is all grim and grudging with little measure of grace, we need a fresh beginning or another calling.

Pablo Casals claimed that "one's work should be a salute to life."[18] The explorer Wilfred Grenfell said that genuine joy grows not from riches or fame, but from work that has its own inner value. Should it be any different for preachers?

Recall the possible thrills related to the preaching task. Do you like learning new words and combinations, alliterations, images, metaphors, and a variety of literary devices? Preaching is a wordsmith's dream. In recollecting his fascination with ministers while yet a youth in his hometown, Harvey Cox relates, "They had huge collections of books and were actually *paid* to read them. . . ."[19]

Do you enjoy detective stories or at least pursuing a puzzling path as far as it goes? Exegetical work will beckon your curiosity. I call it sensing and sleuthing the text. Sensing the text calls for the reading aloud and hearing of the text from several translations; free association of thought and feeling with the text; entering into informal conversation of questioning and being questioned; imagining and intuiting what the text is all about and what gospel is being spoken. Sleuthing the text is tracing out the leads provided in the literary, historical, and form contexts. Imaged as homiletical detective work the task takes on an air of mystery and challenge rather than the sterility of a purely academic enterprise. In addition we become connected in time and empathy with past generations of the faith community.

Does your imagination respond to the challenge of a message being shaped out of a biblical text? Here is your chance. The text will speak for itself. Yet the plain fact is that even as we avoid the rhetorical argument style of classical preaching which preys on the text rather than praying and proceeding from the text, the preacher still has to make theological and interpretive decisions about sermon substance and content. If you want to be a biblically based primary theologian of the people and for the people, preaching will bring its own reward.

Not a few preachers find the act of delivery to be the high in the whole continuum of homiletics. It is the main event toward which all the preparatory discipline is aimed. It is live drama in the arena of worship, the living interaction between God and the faith community. An incomparable "aha experience" takes place for the preacher when a given sermon somehow becomes the Word of God in this time and place for this gathered congregation.

The excitement is hidden in the process, waiting to be discovered and unleashed. After all, should not uncovering the best news in history be the occasion for joyful discovery?

To Be a Messenger
of Ultimate Love, Joy, and Hope

Although there are many subsidiary themes and subplots throughout Scripture, preachers have one dominant theme. When all is said and done, all roads lead to grace, our theological code word for the reality of God's love in action. To paraphrase the title of Joseph Campbell's *The Hero With a Thousand Faces*,[20] grace is the action of God in a thousand guises. These myriad ways of articulating who God is and what God is doing likewise reveal nuances of the human predicament.

In the human situation of estrangement from self, neighbor, life, and God we preach a disturbing, healing, and reconciling grace. We proclaim the radical truth of God's unconditional and everlasting love and thus the worth of the Down's syndrome child and the bedridden citizens at the nursing home on the outskirts of town. We point to the rule of God with its all-encompassing gift and demand of shalom, justice, cosmic harmony, and well-being in both history and nature.

Our vocabulary of grace and its implications is many-splendored: justification, sanctification, emancipation, liberation, new creation, gift and demand, promise and claim, redemption, salvation, regeneration and renewal, to name a few. These themes and terms take on life as they represent the promise and claim of God in the lives of our listeners today. If anything is clear about preaching, however, it is that we who preach are never "qualified" except by God's grace and power. Only dependence on God's grace in the final analysis can prevent the preacher from being overtaken by either arrogance or despair. On the way to the pulpit, then, pray for passion of heart, clarity of mind, facility of speech and above all, trust in the Word.

To hear the Good News is to be touched by a mysterious lover who calls all life into being, yet is before us and after us; who affirms our worth in spite of our failures, offering new beginnings to all our endings; who undergirds the worst sinner with redeeming love and undermines the best hypocrite with judgment calling for repentance; who beckons us to risk for others, yet gives no worldly guarantee of victory other than the victory of risk-filled truth itself.

In a world of seemingly constant bad news, the Good News we proclaim may be the only hopeful sign seen or heard during a week. Preaching can bring forth latent courage in the life of the listener, an invitation to begin again, a challenge to move toward the suffering of others, a way of finding ourselves in the eternal purposes of God in the here and now. Through hearing the gospel a new freedom to choose is created, and the impossible becomes possible.

Conclusion

The preaching journey from Camelot to Covenant is a weekly challenge presupposing a growth model for both parishioners and preacher. As we have seen, Covenant is always redefining Camelot into a larger vision on behalf of the common good.

The movement from Camelot to Covenant frequently has to do with transforming our individual purposes into community-oriented well-being, or in biblical terms, into participation in the Kingdom or Rule of God. Our yearning for meaningful relationships, good health, and sufficient provisions for food, shelter, and clothing are not contrary to the gospel. The point is that the Covenant calls us to want the fullness of life for *all* people, materially and spiritually, and to order our lives in that direction. And that inevitably means inconvenience, risk, and self-giving freely and intentionally chosen on behalf of others. It also means participating in the life and purpose of God and the fulfillment of our time in history.

My reference to preaching from Camelot to Covenant as a growth model is not intended to bypass the many and varied biblical metaphors for the human situation and God's initiatory and responding action of grace. To the contrary, Camelot is a fertile ground for human isolation, brokenness, arrogance, and apathy, as reflected in the specificity of biblical texts. Likewise the irrepressible love of God is revealed in the ongoing journey from Camelot to Covenant whether as the pardoning of justification, new birth, wholeness, or reconciliation. As God through Jesus Christ draws us into community and participation in the Covenant/Rule of God, the shackles of our separation, our guilt, and our emptiness are overcome in the promise and purpose of God. The biblical texts reveal the nuances of sin and grace in the journey.

Most of our preaching in the "mainline" churches seeks to deepen the spiritual life of the listener and to offer genuine guidance for daily existence. Grace and sin are primarily connected with the personal dimensions of each individual's life. In this perspective the church is a "filling station," as it is frequently put, to renew and re-energize the members of the church for their faithful witness in the world. The appropriation of faith in the lives of church members is no small endeavor and is an essential dimension of biblical preaching. The Covenant includes solace and balm in Gilead as well as a call to let the oppressed go free.

Preaching from Camelot to Covenant emphasizes a costly grace freely given, a grace that beckons and invites us into a social and global vision of life that takes seriously God's purpose for creation and for *all* life within it. Covenant preaching moves beyond individualism of Camelot because even at its best—that is, without intent to harm others and to live a decent life—individualism is less than God's intention for all life to live toward and on behalf of a reconciled community of peace and justice. The call to community is not a denial of individual worth but rather an affirmation of responsible freedom lived for the common good as exemplified by Jesus Christ.

Preaching from Camelot to Covenant calls the church to be more than an aggregate of caring individuals, though that in itself is by no means to be discounted. The gospel calls the church to be a *sign* and an *agent* of the gospel in breaking through the barriers and bondage of race, sex, class, and age, both in its own life and witness and in the world at large. The gospel calls the church to be an *advocate* for "marginalized" people and to take sides on behalf of justice *in the name of God through Jesus Christ.* Can preaching do less?

David Buttrick has stated clearly what is at stake in our preaching:

> . . . If Jesus can do nothing more than to come to our
> hearts while in the world babies starve, then he is scarcely

the savior of all. Second-century Gnostics embraced a personal savior, Jesus, but when it came to world problems they discreetly looked elsewhere. A pulpit which, in its personalism, can offer nothing more than a one-to-one savior is in danger of the same gnostic heresy. The issue is not a matter of homiletic preference; the issue is the theological status of Jesus Christ. Because the pulpit in recent American history has been consumingly personal, we have an odd result, namely, a nation filled with nice one-to-one Jesus people who will support the most appalling national policies.[1]

I have claimed earlier in the text that preaching creates a fabric of consciousness. Preaching from Camelot to Covenant is announcing God's action in the world and activating our participation in that action. Being faithful to that gift and challenge is the exasperation and exhilaration of preaching from Camelot to Covenant. So take courage and preach the gospel!

Notes

Chapter 1

1. Justo Gonzalez and Catherine G. Gonzalez, *Liberation Preaching* (Nashville: Abingdon Press, 1980).

2. Dietrich Bonhoeffer, *The Cost of Discipleship*, Revised edition (New York: Macmillan, 1963). See especially Ch. 1 "Costly Grace," pp. 45–60.

3. Elizabeth Achtemeier, *Preaching as Theology and Art* (Nashville: Abingdon Press, 1984), p. 54. The assumption of a readily identifiable, normative biblical and theological tradition continues on pp. 55–56.

4. See also Kenneth L. Gibble, *The Preacher as Jacob, A New Paradigm for Preaching* (Minneapolis: Seabury Press, 1985). Although my own formulations are not indebted to Gibble's work, I wish to express appreciation for his approach and to note the similarities to some degree in our concerns.

5. Elie Wiesel, *Messengers of God* (New York: Summit Books, 1976), pp. 106–9. See "And Jacob Fought the Angel," pp. 103–35.

6. Gerhard Von Rad, *Genesis*, The Old Testament Library (Philadelphia: Westminster Press, 1961).

7. Walter Brueggemann, *Interpretation: A Bible Commentary for Teaching and Preaching* (Atlanta: John Knox, 1982), p. 266.

8. Elie Wiesel, op. cit., p. 107.

9. *The Methodist Hymnal*, "O God of Earth and Altar" (Nashville: Methodist Publishing House, 1964), p. 484.

10. If you are an Arthurian scholar, or an avid devotee of the late John Kennedy, do not take my Camelot too literally. Give me a little "preacherly license."

11. Saint Augustine, *On Christian Doctrine*, translated by D. W. Robertson, Jr. (Indianapolis and New York: The Library of Liberal Arts, 1958), an epigram from Martial to Fidentius, in slightly altered form, translator's preface, p. v.

12. Dietrich Bonhoeffer, *Letters and Papers from Prison*, Eberhard Bethge, ed. (New York: Macmillan, 1953).

13. In her book *Patriarchy as a Conceptual Trap* (Wellesley, MA: Roundtable Press, 1982), Elizabeth Dodson Gray describes a conceptual trap to be like a room with no windows. There are, supposedly, no other possibilities or alternatives. Reality has been named and is in place. There is only one way of looking at things and understanding them.

14. Dorothee Sölle, Lecture Notes, Saint Paul School of Theology.

15. See William K. McElvaney, *Good News Is Bad News Is Good News* (Maryknoll NY: Orbis Books, 1980).

16. Robert McAfee Brown, *Creative Dislocation—The Movement of Grace* (Nashville: Abingdon Press, 1980).

17. Frederick Buechner, *The Magnificent Defeat* (San Francisco: Harper & Row, 1985).

18. *The Book of Worship for Church and Home* (Nashville: Methodist Publishing House, 1964), pp. 382–88.

19. Ibid.

20. For this section I have relied on Volume I, *The Interpreters' Dictionary of the Bible* (Nashville: Abingdon Press, 1962), pp. 722–23, and *Theological Dictionary of the New Testament*, Geoffrey W. Bromiley, translator; Gerhard Kittel and Gerhard Friedrich, eds. (Grand Rapids, MI: William B. Eerdmans, 1985), pp. 160–61.

21. *Interpreters' Dictionary of the Bible*, p. 722

22. *Theological Dictionary of the New Testament*, p. 161.

23. Ibid. p. 161.

Chapter 2

1. Walter Brueggemann, "The Social Nature of Biblical Text," in Arthur Van Seters, *Preaching as a Social Act* (Nashville: Abingdon Press, 1988), p. 143.

2. Ibid., p. 144.

3. William K. McElvaney, op. cit.

4. Mortimer Arias, *Announcing the Reign of God* (Philadelphia: Fortress Press, 1984), p. xv.

5. Ibid., pp. 66–67.

6. Ibid., pp. 67.

7. William Butler Yeats, "The Magi," in *The Collected Poems of W. B. Yeats* (London: Macmillan, 1958), p. 141.

8. Thomas N. Troeger, "The Social Power of Myth as Key to Preaching on Social Issues," in Van Seters, *Preaching as a Social Act*, p. 206.

9. Arias, op. cit., p. 116

10. Martin Luther King, Jr., "The Man Who Was a Fool," in *Strength to Love* (Philadelphia: Fortress Press, 1963), p. 70.

11. J. D. Salinger, *Franny and Zooey* (Boston: Little and Brown, 1955), pp. 147–48.

12. Ronald J. Allen, "The Social Function of Language in Preaching," in Van Seters, *Preaching as a Social Act*, p. 176.

13. William K. McElvaney, op. cit.

14. Letty Russell, recollection from personal conversation.

15. Robert McAfee Brown, op. cit.

Chapter 3

1. Merrill R. Abbey, *The Epic of United Methodist Preaching* (Lanham, MD: University Press of America, 1984), p. 105, quoted from Robert D. Clark, *The Life of Matthew Simpson* (New York: Macmillan, 1956) p. 160.

2. Walter Brueggemann, "The Social Nature of the Biblical Text for Preaching," in Arthur Van Seters, *Preaching as a Social Act* (Nashville: Abingdon Press, 1988), p. 147.

3. For an insightful comparison of the Hebrew prophets with today's preacher, see Walter J. Burghardt, S. J., *Preaching: The Art and the Craft* (New York: Paulist Press, 1987), especially Ch. 3, "Shudder, You Complacent Ones," pp. 29–41. Burghardt acknowledges indebtedness to Abraham J. Heschel's *The Prophets* (Philadelphia: Jewish Publication Society of America, 1962).

4. Harry Huebner, "Peacemaking and the Prophetic Imagination," *The Mennonite*, January 27, 1987, p. 28. Huebner acknowledges indebtedness to Walter Brueggemann's *The Prophetic Imagination* (Philadelphia: Fortress, 1978).

5. This section and some of the material following is indebted to my article, "Speaking Out From the Pulpit," *The Christian Ministry*, May 1982, pp. 5–8.

6. Arthur Van Seters, op. cit., p. 265.

7. Ronald J. Sider and Michael A. King, *Preaching About Life in a Threatening World* (Philadelphia: Westminster Press, 1987), p. 74.

8. Walter J. Burghardt, S. J., op. cit., pp. 39–40.

9. Lee S. Moorehead, *Freedom of the Pulpit* (Nashville: Abingdon Press, 1961), p. 74.

10. Gerhard Ebeling, *The Nature of Faith* (Philadelphia: Muhlenberg Press, 1961), p. 83.

11. Dieter T. Hessel, ed., *Social Themes of the Christian Year* (Philadelphia: Geneva Press, 1983).

12. Ibid., p. 22.

13. Ibid., p. 25.

14. In his book *Design for Preaching*, H. Grady Davis offers the distinction between a text as source and as resource. (Philadelphia: Muhlenberg Press, 1958), p. 47.

15. Leander Keck, *The Bible and the Pulpit* (Nashville: Abingdon Press, 1978), p. 11.

16. Peter Berger, "The Class Struggle in American Religion," *Christian Century*, Feb. 28, 1981, p. 196.

17. Harold A. Bosley, *Preaching on Controversial Issues* (New York: Harper and Brothers, 1953), p. 23.

18. William J. Carl III, *Preaching Christian Doctrine* (Philadelphia: Fortress Press, 1983), p. 121.

19. Ibid., pp. 121–25.

20. James R. Brockman, *The Word Remains, A Life of Oscar Romero* (Maryknoll, NY: Orbis Books, 1982), p. 217.

Chapter 4

1. World Council of Churches, "A Worship book for the Sixth Assembly of the World Council of Churches" (Geneva: W.C.C., 1983). The phrases constitute the theme of the Sixth Assembly, Vancouver, Canada, 1983.

2. Ibid., biblical affirmations for worship, p. 3.

3. Based on numerous personal conversations and on surveys available to the Association of United Methodist Theological Schools.

4. In *Habits of the Heart* Robert Bellah, et al. (Berkeley, CA: University of California Press, 1985), have articulated in some detail the utilitarian and expressive forms of individualism which characterize our North American society. It is worth noting that these authors from the fields of sociology, philosophy, and theology have allowed their subtitle to read "Individualism and Commitment in *American* Life" rather than *North* American Life as though there were no *Central* or *South* America.

5. See David S. Barrett, ed., "Christianity in the Twentieth Century," in *World Christian Encyclopedia* (New York: Oxford University Press, 1982).

6. Omer Degrijse, *Going Forth: Missionary Consciousness in Third World Catholic Churches*, paraphrased by the author (Maryknoll, NY: Orbis Books, 1977).

7. W. Richey Hogg, "God's Mission—Our Ministry," SMU Minister's Week Lecture, 1985.

8. Kosuke Koyama, Iliff Week Graduate Lecture, Jan. 1987.

9. Charles Wesley, "Love Divine, All Loves Excelling," *Methodist Hymnal* (Nashville: Methodist Publishing House, 1964), p. 283.

10. Massey Shepherd, Jr., *Liturgy and Education* (New York: Seabury Press, 1967), p. 110.

11. Elsa Tamez, "Come and Celebrate the Supper of the Lord," in Cancionero Abierto, *Confessing Our Faith Around the World*, Faith and Order Paper #123 (III), (Geneva: W.C.C., 1984), p. 17. Written in 1982 by Elsa Tamez, a biblical scholar at the Latin America Biblical Seminary. This poem, which is already widely used in various churches, especially for the celebration of the Eucharist, was set to music by Pablo Sosa from Argentina.

12. See *Social Themes of the Christian Year*, Dieter T. Hessel, ed. (Philadelphia: Geneva Press, 1983), also recommended in my Ch. 4.

13. Robert McAfee Brown, *Unexpected News* (Philadelphia: Westminster Press, 1984), pp. 135–36.

Chapter 5

1. A Letter from Roselyn Elliott, July 18, 1985, used by permission.

2. William Blake, "Auguries of Innocence" ll. 59–62. *The Complete Writings of William Blake*, Geoffrey Keynes, ed. (London: The Nonesuch Press, 1957).

3. James S. Stewart, *Heralds of God* (New York: Scribner's, 1946), p. 46.

4. Hans Van Der Geest, *Presence in the Pulpit* (Atlanta: John Knox Press, 1981). Research by Van Der Geest indicates that the content of the preacher's work has significance only in the framework of the relationship between preacher and congregation. As he puts it, "The effect of a textual explanation is inextricably associated with the effect of the preacher . . . the truth is not cognitive, but rather communicative" (p. 61). In my opinion this is essential to take into consideration even though I regard it as a partial truth.

5. Margaret Craven, *I Heard the Owl Call My Name* (Garden City, NY: Doubleday, 1973).

6. Alex Haley, *Roots* (Garden City, NY: Doubleday, 1976).

7. Robert Bellah, et al., *Habits of the Heart* (Berkeley, CA: University of California Press, 1985), Ch. 6, "Individualism," p. 154.

8. Martin Luther, *A Commentary on St. Paul's Epistle to the Galatians*, translated by Theodore Graebner, 4th ed. (Grand Rapids, MI: Zondervan Publishing House, n.d.), p. 242.

9. In *The Philosophy of Moral Development* (San Francisco: Harper & Row, 1981) Lawrence Kohlberg articulates six stages of moral development. Through her book *In a Different Voice*

(Cambridge, MA: Harvard University Press, 1982) Carol Gilligan broadens the base of moral development by contrasting female and male patterns. James Fowler explores six stages of faith development in his book *Stages of Faith* (San Francisco: Harper & Row, 1981). A reading of these sources contributes to the preacher's awareness of the variety of hearers occupying the pew on Sunday.

10. Adapted from William K. McElvaney, *The People of God in Ministry* (Nashville: Abingdon, 1981), p. 22.

11. Pablo Casals, *Joys and Sorrows.* His own story as told to Albert E. Kahn (New York: Simon and Schuster, 1970), p. 105.

12. See *As One Without Authority,* Fred B. Craddock, 3rd ed., (Nashville: Abingdon, 1983), especially "The Pulpit in the Shadows," pp. 1–21.

Chapter 6

1. C. S. Lewis, *Screwtape Letters* (New York: Macmillan, 1953).

2. Gary Johnson, "Isaiah Resembling," text originally set to music (Saint Paul School of Theology, 1984), used by permission.

3. James R. Brockman, S. J., *The Word Remains: A Life of Oscar Romero* (Maryknoll, NY: Orbis Books, 1982), cover statement.

4. Ronald E. Sleeth, *Proclaiming the Word* (Nashville: Abingdon Press, 1964), pp. 13–30.

5. Merrill R. Abbey, *The Epic of United Methodist Preaching* (Lanham, MD: University Press of America, 1984), p. xiv.

6. Clyde E. Fant, *Preaching for Today* (New York: Harper & Row, 1975), p. 24.

7. Ibid., p. 26.

8. Gardner Taylor, "Shaping Sermons by the Shape of Text and Preacher," in *Preaching Biblically,* D. M. Wardlaw, ed. (Philadelphia: Westminster Press, 1983).

9. Bernard Manning, quoted by Gardner Taylor, op. cit.

10. James Wharton, "An Eschatological Laundry List of Unscientific Prescripts About What Preaching Is," unpublished tract, Sept. 12, 1986.

11. See Fred B. Craddock, *As One Without Authority,* 3rd ed. (Nashville: Abingdon Press, 1983), especially "The Pulpit in the Shadows," pp. 1–21.

12. See Craddock, op. cit. and Ronald Sleeth, *God's Word and Our Words* (Atlanta: John Knox Press, 1986). Reference is made to the works of Walter J. Ong, Frank Dance, Susanne K. Langer, Marshall McLuhan, Robert W. Funk, among others.

13. Richard L. Eslinger, *A New Hearing* (Nashville: Abingdon Press, 1987), p. 142. The original source quoted is Buttrick's paper,

"The Powers That Be, Revisited," delivered at the Hickman Lectures, Duke University Divinity School Convocation, Durham, NC, October 23, 1979.

14. Sally McFague, "Between Athens and Jerusalem: The Seminary in Tension," *Christian Century*, February 4–11, 1976, 90–92.

15. This section on archetypes for all types is paraphrased and extended from William K. McElvaney, *The People of God in Ministry* (Nashville: Abingdon, 1981), pp. 48–51.

16. Merrill Abbey, *The Word Interprets Us* (Nashville: Abingdon Press: 1967).

17. Walter Burghardt, *Still Proclaiming Your Wonders* (New York: Paulist Press, 1984).

18. Fritz Henle, *Casals* (New York: American Photographic Book Publishing Co., 1975).

19. Harvey Cox, *The Seduction of the Spirit* (New York: Simon & Schuster, 1973), p. 44.

20. Joseph Campbell, *The Hero With a Thousand Faces*, Bollingen Series XVII (Princeton, NJ: Princeton University Press, 1949).

Conclusion

1. David G. Buttrick, *Homiletic* (Philadelphia: Fortress Press, 1987), p. 421.

251
M14/

80536

LINCOLN CHRISTIAN COLLEGE AND SEMINARY